W9-BHN-048

Elderhostels

Elderhostels

The Students' Choice

Mildred Hyman

John Muir Publications
Santa Fe, New Mexico

John Muir Publications, P.O. Box 613, Santa Fe, NM 87504

© 1989 by Mildred Hyman
Cover © 1989 by John Muir Publications
All rights reserved. Published 1989
Printed in the United States of America

First edition. First printing

Library of Congress Cataloging-in-Publication Data
Hyman, Mildred L., 1920-
  Elderhostels: the students' choice / Mildred Hyman. —1st ed.
    p. cm.
  ISBN 0-945465-28-9
  1. Aged—Education. 2. Adult education—Curricula. 3. College
facilities—Extended use. I. Title.
LC 5457.H93 1989
374'.01—dc20
                                               89-42939
                                                  CIP

Typeface: Century Schoolbook
Typesetter: Copygraphics, Inc.
Designer: Mary Shapiro
Printer: McNaughton-Gunn

Distributed to the book trade by:
W.W. Norton & Company, Inc.
New York, New York

Contents

Foreword

When I discovered that the text herein by my fellow Tucsonan Mildred Hyman has good descriptions about accommodations available for Elderhostelers in their travels, I was reminded of my 1976 presidential campaign. You may remember that in the early days of the campaign, my chief opponent, Jimmy Carter, a good ol' boy, ran kind of a down-home type of operation. He did things like stay in people's homes as he traveled back and forth across the country. "You've got to do that, too," said my key advisers. "It'll make you more human. Besides, we'll save a few bucks." I probably was more impressed by the second argument, but anyway, I agreed to give it a try. Now my 6'-5" frame is not easily parked, and I wound up one night sleeping, or trying to sleep, in a bed usually occupied by my host's small daughter. It was a miserable night. "No more," I told the staff the next morning. "Let Jimmy Carter have any votes he can get that way."

That's kind of an oblique way of making a point here—that *Elderhostels: The Students' Choice* would seem to be must reading for those of you who frequently travel to unfamiliar places and want to know what to expect when you arrive. Obviously, the quality of the educational experience is of top priority. But comfort is important, too. The need for a book frankly discussing Elderhostel offerings is obvious. Institutions aren't going to emphasize the shortcomings of their programs, educational or otherwise. I have a friend who went to a New England resort whose brochure said the beach was only a short walk through "field and pine." It turned out to be a horrible two-mile hike through a brier patch. Mildred says the program at my alma mater, the University of Arizona in Tucson, has teachers who are well prepared and know their subjects. But she says the accommodations "leave much to be desired." So be it. Elderhosteling will be much less guesswork to readers of this book.

Morris K. Udall
Member of Congress

Acknowledgments

I am sincerely grateful to the contributors to this work. Without their earnest assistance, this guide would not have been possible. Thanks to them, it is an engaging mix of kudos and complaints, congratulations and criticism.

My panel of sixty-one Elderhostelers are a geographically diverse group, from urban, suburban, and rural locations in some twenty-six states. Many interviews were conducted face-to-face, but the majority of evaluations were solicited through the mail. My one-in-five response was far superior to any direct-mail response received during my professional career (as a director of development). Obviously, soliciting information is easier than soliciting funds. This method, however, resulted in some institutions receiving less extensive treatment than I would have liked. I will try to rectify this problem in the next edition.

This acknowledgment would be incomplete without thanking my conscientious editors, whose patience must have been taxed by my computer illiteracy.

Introduction

The Elderhostel organization, founded in 1975, has been called the greatest social movement of the century by *Time* magazine. Headquartered in Boston, Massachusetts, it is based on the premise that people of all ages should have access to education. Founder Marty Knowlton, a social activist and educator, patterned his program on the European youth hostel movement. Like the European model, there is no charge for membership and the organization is nonprofit. Many golden-agers would dispute the adage that life begins at forty—for them, through Elderhosteling, it begins at sixty.

Over twelve hundred institutions in fifty-one states and forty foreign countries offer a variety of one-to-three-week residential educational programs. Major universities, community colleges, music schools, conference centers, and national parks are among the ever-increasing number of host institutions. Elderhostel courses are not for credit, and, except for a few intensive study programs, there are no exams, grades, or required assignments.

Six times a year (a special winter supplement made it seven in 1988) thousands of men and women over age sixty receive, at no cost, large newsprint catalogs of educational opportunities. That official catalog contains a ten- to-twelve-line description of each facility, followed by a brief summary of the courses and schedule of dates the course is given. This is not a great deal of information, particularly for the first-time hosteler.

The catalog contains an array of appealing opportunities, but it can be a surfeit of riches. With so many offerings, how can the novice Elderhosteler select the destination that will best meet his or her special interests and physical needs? Because the catalog descriptions are written by the host institutions, it is unlikely that their own shortcomings and weaknesses will be revealed. Some colleges, struggling to keep their fiscal heads above water, burdened by escalating costs, declining enrollments, and diminished financial aid, have turned to Elderhosteling to fill unused classrooms and dorms. These schools are not apt to be forthright about their frugal cafeterias or the inhospitality of their terrain. How, then, can the prospective attendees learn what any given site or program "is really like?"

The need for this guide surfaced about five years ago when I, too, started to Elderhostel. I found myself, like many new to the movement, cross-examining the old hands at every opportunity. Table conversation in the cafeteria at breakfast, lunch, and dinner revolved primarily around previous Elderhostel experiences. I took numerous mental notes but forgot the details ("All New England sites fill to capacity early in the fall foliage season. Santa Fe is a must for opera buffs, but not if you're a hearty eater."). It soon became clear that I should keep an Elderhostel journal.

I recently met a forty-year-old woman who volunteers as a docent at the Arizona Desert Museum. When I mentioned my Elderhosteling to her, she looked at me with new respect and laughed. "My trainer at the museum warned me," she said. "Tour all the little fifth-grade classes you can get, but never, never, never host a group of Elderhostelers. They know more than you do about your subject and aren't the least bit shy about telling you so."

The young woman's statement triggered the thought that those unshy Elderhostelers must return some very provocative evaluations to their host institutions along with their room keys at the conclusion of their stay. I thought, wouldn't those uncensored comments be fun to read! I was right. They are fun to read—and informative, too. Rumors like the one voiced by the museum trainer may have given rise to the cliché opprobrium "hostile elders." But the opprobrium is undeserved; for the most part, you will find the reviews that follow to be frank but also tolerant.

Our need for information seems to be similar to that of the eighteen-year-old prospective college student who selects his destination after a fact-finding campus visit, a chat with students, an audit of classes, and a stroll of the neighboring community. That high school senior has another advantage over the Elderhosteler— access to dozens of college guidebooks that list the "most popular, most exciting and the best." Some published college guides rate schools by cost and SATs required. Elderhosteling costs are modest and the only SAT score necessary is your word as to your age and a desire to learn something you have always dreamed of learning, or a wish to hear again something half-forgotten.

This book, much like the underground student guides, contains candid program critiques submitted by experienced Elderhostelers for the use of the uninitiated. Most of all, this travel guide has been compiled to take the place of that campus visit. Although it would be impossible for me to determine "the best" or "most exciting" program, those adjectives have been used occasionally by the contributors. But I note the "most popular" institutions when informed about long waiting lists. Under the "Getting In" category, I warn my readers about overpopular programs and the need for early registration.

But early registration is not the whole answer. The most popular programs cannot be filled on a simple first-come, first-served basis out of fear that Bostonians would get preferential treatment by hand delivering their requests. Therefore, when applications exceed available space, a computer-generated lottery is held one month after the catalog is delivered to determine the accepted registrants and the waiting lists. During summer 1988, Elderhostel's national registration department received 400 applications for an Alaskan program that had space for fifty. This little-known, random-selection process does not seem to be discouraging Elderhostelers, who continue to join the movement in droves. My best guess is that only a handful of the available twelve hundred destinations must be filled by lottery.

When I tried to register for an East Coast program in December 1988, I was placed in a new nonenrolled category, "wait-list and standby." My registration certificate was wrapped in a packet of goldenrod and pink form letters that explained my options and the necessary procedures. Elderhostel standby, like the airline classification of the same name, is designed for travelers free to take off on a moment's notice. This was not an option open to me, but the use of a standby process reveals the organization's efforts to solve its serious registration difficulties.

Cost is not a factor at Elderhostels—the weekly rate varies only by five or ten dollars. The cost in the United States is typically $235 per week for room, board, and no more than three classes, each of which meets for one to one and a half hours per weekday. That fee includes registration, six nights' lodging, all meals from Sunday evening through the following Saturday breakfast, five days of classes, and some field trips and extracurricular activities. The cost and arrangements for travel to and from your destination in the United States, Canada, Jamaica, Mexico, and Bermuda are your own responsibility.

The difficulty of traveling to and from some locations is infrequently, if ever, mentioned in the catalog. Driving alone, I have struggled with treacherous mountain roads and axle-breaking unpaved furrows so rough I would have reconsidered or made other travel arrangements had I been forewarned. In addition, lodgings vary from college dormitories to luxury hotels with private baths, and from bunk beds in youth hostels to private homes in foreign countries. The variety of housing accommodations is not adequately addressed in the official catalog. Even the tableware varies from tin mess kits to silver teapots. The most common misconception among nonmembers is that Elderhosteling is not for them. They find the prospect of sharing a bathroom and eating institutional food displeasing. As you will learn in the following pages, fancy amenities such as private baths and gourmet food are available at some destinations.

In compiling this work, I was awed by the eclectic range of programs and people. Hostelers wade through Chomskyan linguistic theory in Massachusetts, write poetry in Iowa, and debate religious philosophy in an air-conditioned classroom overlooking Mulholland Drive. But the classrooms are not all indoors. Hostelers photograph Alaskan glaciers and spot bighorn sheep in virgin forests. Nor do the classes appeal only to philosophy scholars. Elderhosteling appeals to people with the time and intellectual curiosity to know the woods and wilderness firsthand and to value the flora and fauna found there. These environmentally concerned Elderhostelers worry about leaving their grandchildren and great-grandchildren a diminished world whose natural beauty and vitality have been exploited.

Not only do the intellectual interests of hostelers vary, but their physical and social needs are also diverse. The sixty-year-old, still active in a career, has needs unlike those of a septuagenarian or an octogenarian. The social differences are those of a generation; the sixty-year-old born in the Depression year of 1929 may have few memories in common with the ninety-year-old born in 1899 before McKinley was shot. Everyone over age sixty is not exactly a contemporary.

And that dissimilitude of people and programs prevented me from designing a system to rank Elderhostels. When it was suggested that the book be subtitled *The Best and the Worst*, it was OK with me, but it was not OK with many Elderhostelers. Most of my fellow members proved to be proud and protective. I was told, "There are no worst." I always had to promise anonymity and occasionally had to repeat my inquiry to elicit specific criticisms from my contributors. I often said, "Think of yourself as a not-young woman traveling alone, or a newcomer to the movement. Which destinations should they avoid?" Not surprisingly, the same complaints were echoed over and over about the same institutions.

Favorites were easy to spot. I asked contributors to submit evaluations of a few of their most positive and negative experiences, and of the thousands of possible destinations, I found the same schools surfaced repeatedly. Included herein are the results of that unscientific selection. You will find many direct quotes from Elderhostelers who have returned to the same host institution four and five times. Yes, the quotes are subjective, but no more so than those in any other insider's travel book.

I did not design a system to rank programs, but a man who did, a man "hooked on Elderhostel" who ranked his thirty experiences on a scale of one to five, shared his chart with me. All of his number one favorites are also praised by the panelists. The man, probably a statistician or actuary before retirement, mails his chart and newsletter to Elderhostel acquaintances.

This was not developed as a "kiss and tell" exposé, a "let's-accept-the-host's-hospitality-then-give-'em-a-black-eye" sort of inside scoop, albeit some institutions seem to deserve a shiner. But please remember that the deficiencies may have been corrected since publication of this book. I urge readers to call the Elderhostel director at the site before registering to determine if the problem reported herein has been rectified. Despite all my years of research and efforts to update the facts, things change. The educational institutions that host Elderhostel programs are not static. Institutions grow and improve: universities can clean their dormitories and hire new chefs, and, conversely, they can go downhill and cut back existing services. Railroad companies and airlines may cancel unprofitable stops. One Elderhostel addict noted unhappily that when she registered for a third year at a favorite destination, she was told the school van that had formerly met her at the airport would not be available this year. She was advised that this time she should try to share the $22.00 taxi ride from the airport to her dormitory.

I have tried to avoid a dull, mathematical comparison of places and services, but I have included some numbers that seem relevant. For instance, the size of the school: huge Ann Arbor with its 34,000 students has a campus environment vastly different from the University of New England with its 600 undergraduates. I have also indicated the altitude of many sites. A physician warned me that the decreased oxygen of high elevations may cause pulmonary or cerebral edema in some elderly folk.

As egalitarian as Elderhostel purports to be, it nevertheless has developed its own social stratification based on the number of hostels attended. Except for this one infraction, the populist philosophy seems to work. Snobbery of any stripe is discouraged. The retired ditchdigger rooms with the retired bank president, and the former manicurist stands in the cafeteria line with the former school principal. With just eight Elderhostel notches in my gun, I have roomed with a former magazine editor, a retired dancer, and a former nonprofit executive. I have square danced with a telephone lineman, scooped ice cream with a retired farmer, listened to opera with a college administrator, and photographed a Hohokam burial site with a retired nuclear physicist. But information about former careers and curriculum vitae just trickle forth over bowls of chocolate pudding.

While gathering material for this book, I conducted a face-to-face interview with a married couple who had experienced a particularly dismal hostel. After commiserating with the unhappy pair, I asked, "Did you complete your postsession evaluation form honestly? That's your tool for calling the administration to task." The woman replied angrily, "No, because I knew the program director would just toss our evaluation into the round file, since she was responsible for our displeasure." I pressed, "Then why didn't you forward your complaints to Boston headquarters?" The husband sighed. "We didn't want Boston to penalize us regarding future requests. Put us down as cranks. We've been on a couple of waiting lists."

I hope this little book will lessen the number of such unfortunate episodes. By shopping carefully for their destinations, readers will be able to separate the wheat from the chaff and increase their odds of having a truly rewarding experience. I hope this opinionated journey reads like a dialogue with a friend.

The Students' Choice

Alaska

Anchorage—Alaska-Pacific University

Courses of Study: Flora and Fauna of Alaska; Art; Photography

Quality of Instructors: The reviewers found the instruction adequate at best and poor at worst.

Environment: Anchorage is the only program of the 100-plus we reviewed for which I was unable to obtain a consensus of opinion. One couple were so cold in Anchorage that they shivered at the memory. They admitted that "trying to get warm" cast their entire experience in a negative light. "Alaska is BIG and Anchorage a bleak city of 300,000 people," they said. However, a conflicting report described Anchorage in the summer as a riot of color, with peonies the size of grapefruit. One enthusiastic couple said the highlight of their week was renting bicycles and exploring the lovely public parks.

It was agreed by all reviewers that Anchorage is not an inviting little college town—it is Alaska's largest city.

Housing: Inadequate for the intensity of the cold climate. In August the radiators are turned off in the dorms, and only one blanket per bed is issued.

Food: "Bad," complained one discontented pair of veteran hostelers. "A gastronomic disaster."

Unique Attributes: The staff members are friendly and arrange good side trips to see salmon fishing and mining. You might even see huge Kodiak bears.

"The best part of our Alaskan trip was the week we spent on our own. We went to Fairbanks and took a river trip to see blue glaciers, alpine peaks, and icebergs that looked like natural ice sculptures. We've heard that the Sitka Elderhostel program is excellent." Not so odd, since Sitka is an Indian name that means "the best place."

The bars stay open until 5 a.m. in this macho state. And do not forget all those extra hours of daylight because of Alaska's proximity to the Arctic Circle. Reading about it is not the same as experiencing this delightful phenomenon.

Shortcomings: Too cold. The weather can be foggy and misty in August. "Alaska is big and so are its mosquitoes, and they have lots of them!" "Give it back to the Eskimos." A much-traveled Elderhostel couple voted this their most unpleasant experience. When interviewed they had attended sixteen hostels.

Getting In: In spite of the expensive airfare, the Alaskan programs have become, according to my reporters, the "most popular." During the summer of 1988, some Alaskan programs had to be filled by computer lottery as described in the introduction.

Getting There: Anchorage can be reached by regularly scheduled airlines.

Arizona

Cordes Junction—Arcosanti

Courses of Study: The Urban Laboratory; Arcosanti Design; Architecture and Cosmology

Quality of Instructors: Dedicated experts-in-residence teach geology, land use, architecture, and cosmology. The lectures are augmented with slides, films, and hands-on experiences. I only received one complaint—that the lesson pertaining to the evolution of the planet was difficult to follow.

Environment: Arcosanti is a relatively isolated, unfinished urban laboratory sixty-five miles north of Phoenix. It is the design, planned habitat, and vision of the brilliant, radical architect, Paolo Soleri. Domed concrete structures in various stages of completeness sit on the crest and side of a spectacular mesa. Experimental solar greenhouses and a working forge (kept busy casting Soleri bells) are also part of the complex.

Cordes Junction is located halfway between Phoenix and Flagstaff. The 3,800-foot altitude creates a climate brisk in winter and pleasant in the summer.

Housing: Elderhostelers stay in twin-bedded rooms with private baths in a small motellike building at the base of a steep hill. The quarters are spartan and a tough climb away from the dining area. Individual gas space heaters are welcome on chilly nights.

Food: Adequate, but no choice of menu is offered in the small cafeteria. The meals are geared more to the taste and needs of the young, resident construction workers than to the needs of senior citizens. Members of the resident staff operate a bakery on an upper level of the visitors center and the tantalizing fragrances of fresh-baked bread and cinnamon cookies fill the dining room each morning.

Unique Attributes: Have you ever eaten frugal soup? One of the thought-provoking activities scheduled at Paolo Soleri's futuristic city is a weekly picnic in the Boschetto, where visitors and staff share thoughts, experiences, and readings about world hunger. The picnic is but one of several dialogues Elderhostelers have with Signore Soleri during which he shares his imaginative philosophy and complex concept of arcology. "We even received a glossary of key words and ideas upon arrival." "One of the most unusual and informative weeks I've ever spent in Elderhosteling." "Definitely a program for the intellectually curious."

Guided nature hikes to Indian ruins, Hohokam burial grounds, and petroglyphs are conducted by exceptionally talented geographers, historians, and naturalists, but they are for robust hikers only.

Shortcomings: Arcosanti is a construction site in use, and therefore the terrain is very rugged; stairs and gravel paths make it a challenge. The campus coordinator's letter is very clear and warns attendees about the rough dirt road that leads into the property—it is a

Visitor center café, Arcosanti, Arizona.

Silt-casting, Arcosanti.

Signore Soleri and Elderhostelers at Arcosanti.

three-mile, axle-breaking stretch. A communal room is needed for between- and after-class socializing. Until then, you had better bring a radio, good book, or knitting to while away long evenings in your neat, recently constructed, bare-bones motel room.

"I attended during Arcosanti's second year of Elderhosteling. I hope they can achieve a better nutritional balance in the future." The program coordinator is just learning about the needs of Elderhostelers.

Getting In: Arcosanti can only accommodate sixteen Elderhostelers, so getting in is rather difficult.

Getting There: This program is accessible only by automobile or bus from Phoenix or Flagstaff to Cordes Junction. The program coordinator will arrange to meet the bus at Cordes Junction.

Flagstaff—Northern Arizona University

Courses of Study: Southwest Archaeology: The Spanish Southwest; Yoga; The Anasazi Indians; The Grand Canyon: The World's Greatest Natural Wonder

Quality of Instructors: All instructors receive an excellent to superb rating.

Environment: NAU has a large, beautiful campus in the heart of northern Arizona sight-seeing territory. Flagstaff is the crossroads, the jumping-off place to see

the red rocks of Sedona, a few miles south, and Walnut
Creek Canyon to the east.

Flagstaff is located in the Coconino National Forest at
an elevation of 7,000 feet. It is a homely little city, an
ugly duckling surrounded by lovely swans. Approached
from either end, the main street is a forest of neon-lit
motels and fast-food emporiums.

Arizona has twenty Indian reservations, and the Hopi
and Navajo reservations are an easy drive from Flagstaff. Visitors are welcome to drive to the old pueblo
villages on top of the mesas, but guests must be dis-
creet. Photographing, taping, or sketching the native
rituals may be forbidden, and spectators should be
respectfully dressed; no shorts or halter tops are permitted, because some of the performances, like the
Kachina dances, are religious in nature.

Housing: The major source of complaint at the Flagstaff campus seems to be the housing. Several groups of
Elderhostelers housed off-campus in a commercial
motel two miles away from school were disappointed
with rooms that were clean but needed repairs to
plumbing, and so forth. "Our very old dorm at the
northerly edge of the campus was inexcusable," one
couple said. "It was like a disreputable army bar-
racks." Other attendees reported comfortable, adequate accommodations in school dormitories, or in a
motel just a ten-minute walk from campus.

Food: Meals served in the college cafeteria are good to
excellent, but more attention could be paid to house-
keeping details. One motel only serves breakfast, and
the motel used in October 1988 offered three meals a
day, with a fixed, waitress-served menu. The menu,

just for the Elderhostel group, was published at the beginning of the week.

Unique Attributes: The school has a beautiful building on campus that contains an Olympic swimming pool, but one reviewer noted that the program was so full she did not have time to enjoy the pool. The program is very well organized; leaders arrange an ice-breaking get-together the first evening and enough evening activities to forge some group cohesiveness.

"The weather is divine. Cool every night in the summer. The students are very friendly and the local museum is a must!"

The visit to the Lowell Observatory (where the planet Pluto was discovered) is an unusual learning experience. "I saw the rings of Saturn," exclaimed one hosteler.

The all-day trip to the Grand Canyon is the highlight of NAU's program. Every American should at some time in his or her life stand at the top of that great precipice and marvel at the silent beauty of the Colorado River snaking through the valley below.

Shortcomings: Check on your housing accommodations before you register. NAU has only been offering Elderhostel programs since 1986, so the staff is still ironing out the wrinkles. Morton Hall dormitory is a half-mile walk to the cafeteria. This is not a problem if you bring your own automobile.

Getting In: This is a very popular program. It is best to register early.

Getting There: Flagstaff has a Continental Trailways bus terminal, an airport, and is on the mainline of the Santa Fe Railroad. But to enjoy the sight-seeing to its fullest, an automobile is a necessity.

Nogales—University of Arizona

Courses of Study: Border-related subjects; Mexican and Indian Art; History of Cattle Ranching; Southern Arizona Prehistory; Spanish for Travelers

Quality of Instructors: Varies from excellent down to barely adequate.

Environment: Nogales is a small, bustling, commercial city on the Mexican border. It lies in the midst of dry, southwestern hills and gullies that have a stark, parched beauty that is most unusual.

The hotel is a short walk from the border, enabling attendees to wander at will into Mexico across the border to sightsee and shop.

Housing: This Elderhostel provides excellent accommodations in a centrally located hotel.

Food: Excellent food is provided in the hotel dining room. Many authentic Sonoran dishes, of course.

Unique Attributes: The entire event is well run and well organized. Finding an elevator in the hotel is a nice surprise. This a particularly good hostel for individuals curious about Mexico but not quite ready to spend a week on the other side of the border. Nogales, Mexico, provides an interesting contrast to its sister city in Arizona. The Mexican city is a bustling tourist mecca, where crowds of Americans flock to purchase handmade huaraches and pottery, while Nogales, Arizona, is a homely little industrial center whose streets are lined with small motels, factories, and gas stations.

This Elderhostel provides a special opportunity to discuss firsthand the problems of U.S.-Mexican relations.

Shortcomings: Nogales is best reached by private automobile. Getting to Nogales by bus is a trifle awkward. The bus driver is not prepared to let passengers disembark in front of the hotel. Double-check with the bus company before loading your suitcase onto the vehicle.

Getting In: No one reported problems.

Getting There: By private automobile or public bus from Tucson.

Phoenix—Grand Canyon College

Courses of Study: Old Testament History; Advanced Photography; History of Arizona; Be a Clown —The Art and Techniques of Clowning

Quality of Instructors: Reported as average to exceptional.

Environment: The college is located in the heart of Phoenix, a sprawling Southwestern metropolis with palm tree-lined boulevards. The city has a downtown of modern, glass-walled skyscrapers and neighborhoods of white stucco, Spanish-style residences with red terra-cotta half-roofs, surrounded by groves of fragrant citrus trees. The city just spirals out into the desert until its growth is halted by a ring of mountains.

The college has easy access to all city buses, and the college buildings have handicap access. The school is a Christian liberal arts college that maintains a Christian perspective.

Housing: Elderhostelers stay in normal student dormitories with shared bathrooms. Smoking is permitted in restricted areas only.

Food: Excellent meals with a large variety of choices are served in the student cafeteria.

Unique Attributes: Very well planned extracurricular activities are scheduled for all afternoons and evenings. Arrangements are made for Elderhostelers who wish to take advantage of concerts, shows, and other entertainment in town, all easily reached on public buses. There are plenty of after-hour activities in Phoenix and plenty of ways to get there (reasonably priced Mexican restaurants, too). By all means see the Heard Museum of Anthropology and Primitive Art with its spectacular kachina doll and Indian art collections. Elderhostelers are welcome to use the school's heated swimming pool and lighted tennis courts. Phoenix enjoys 300 sunny days per year.

Shortcomings: Only complaint repeated over and over was, "Hard to get in." Beware: The average high temperature June through August is 103 degrees. May and September are almost as bad.

Getting In: This is a popular winter destination. Grand Canyon College Elderhostel program has a long waiting list every January and February.

Getting There: Phoenix has an international airport served by most major airlines and has good public bus service.

Prescott—Yavapai Junior College

Courses of Study: Geology; Arizona History; Spanish Language; Southwest Indian Artifacts; Exploring Red Rock Country

Quality of Instructors: Most of the teachers are lively and interesting. I received complaints about one long-winded professor.

Environment: Prescott is a historic old town located in pine-clad mountains one hundred miles north of Phoenix. From the city, one has a panoramic view of forests of pine, ash, walnut and cherry. The campus is not particularly attractive—"rather ordinary," according to one couple. Prescott is a nontraditional school where environmental studies are an essential component of the curriculum, and undergraduates do extensive field work.

Housing: Elderhostelers stay in dormitories that have small rooms with private baths. The accommodations are given a very good rating, and the private baths are an inducement for many Elderhostelers. When school is in session, Elderhostelers are housed in a nearby motel. Rumor has it that Yavapai is building a new dormitory soon.

Food: The meals at Yavapai are prepared by a concessionaire and could be improved. "Poor quality and poor choices," wrote one reviewer. "No better and no worse than most," wrote another. Meals are served in the student center cafeteria at hours convenient for the preparers and the student athletes, not for Elderhostelers.

Unique Attributes: The field trips to the Grand Canyon or to Sedona/Oak Creek Canyon are wonderful and are included in some programs. A broad variety of entertainment, slide shows, music, and so forth, is arranged for evenings. Prescott is an old mining town and contains some interesting landmarks. Like Flagstaff, the city is ideally located for watching the daylight change and play on some of Arizona's natural wonders—the red rocks of Sedona and the grand cliffs and plateaus of the Grand Canyon. Summer weather is delightful; the days are pleasant and the nights chilly. Springtime, however, can be cold and wet, as one reviewer reported.

With a car, one can take a side trip to Jerome State Historic Park. Jerome became a ghost town in 1953, when the last copper-mining operation closed. All that remains of a bustling mining town are a few residents peddling historical mementos.

Shortcomings: The walk uphill from the dormitories to the classes and cafeteria is very long. Elderhostelers unable to negotiate the hill had better have their own automobiles available. One couple told me that of six Elderhostel experiences, only one, Prescott, needed improvement. The husband, a food chemist, was appalled to find the cooking teacher using raw goat's milk. He mentioned his concern to the program director and also expressed his alarm in writing. The letter was never acknowledged. "Tell your readers not to sign up for the cooking class at Yavapai," he warned.

Getting In: No waiting lists reported.

Getting There: Prescott is best reached by private automobile. To fully enjoy the nearby sights and parks, a car is recommended, although the area is served by tour buses and by Golden Pacific Commuter Airlines.

Tucson—University of Arizona

Courses of Study: History of the American West; Rustlers and Wranglers; Scanning the Silver Screen; Pioneer Jews of the Southwest; Native Americans; Psychology; Genealogy

University of Arizona campus, Tucson. (Photo by Barbara L. Silvers)

Quality of Instructors: The teachers are well prepared and know their subjects.

Environment: The university is spread over an urban campus with approximately 37,000 students and is located in the center of a southwestern city of 600,000 inhabitants.

The predominant architectural style of Tucson is pink Spanish adobe topped with flat roofs and red-tile trim. The smooth stucco facade of the homes and old office buildings create a perfect surface for reflecting the multicolored prisms of the red-orange southwestern sunsets. The Sun Belt city sits in a valley ringed by five ranges of purple mountains, but the Elderhostelers are housed too far away to enjoy either the city or the campus. The main two thoroughfares of the city are a tasteless jungle of billboards and vulgar strips of commercialism.

Housing: The accommodations used for the Elderhostel program leave much to be desired. Various motels have been used, one reported as having all motel services but located in an unsavory, inconvenient neighborhood. Another "downtown" motel used for lodging Elderhostelers has a commanding view of a used-car lot! None are convenient to the university campus.

Food: The food is good and the selection excellent in many of the school cafeterias. Expect to find many Mexican dishes, such as chimis, tacos, and guacamole, since Hispanics comprise 26 percent of Tucson's population. A few evaluators groused about the long lines in the cafeterias; however, a pair of Elderhostel devotees were much-miffed when they had to eat all their meals

Elderhostelers chatting with students, University of Arizona, Tucson. (Photo by Barbara L. Silvers)

Bulletin board of Centennial Hall Theater, University of Arizona, Tucson. (Photo by Barbara L. Silvers)

in the motel with a fixed menu limited to a single entrée. In their view, one of the outstanding features of the Elderhostel experience is the opportunity to have informal dialogue with students in the cafeteria and while walking on the campus between classes.

Unique Attributes: Tucson is a sprawling city and the campus is centered around a spacious green mall where the students hang out in the bright winter sunshine. "I loved the landscaping on the campus and in town. Lots of palm trees, saguaros and many varieties of cacti." The dry desert climate and 360 days of sunshine draw large numbers of Elderhostelers to Tucson in the winter. A few miles to the south one can visit Indian reservations and a Tucson landmark, the serene and beautiful 300-year-old Spanish mission, San Xavier del Bac. All U of A Tucson Elderhostel weeks include a trip to the Arizona-Sonora Desert Museum, one of the greatest natural habitat and educational demonstration museums in the world.

Elderhostelers may be lucky enough to encounter a few real-live cowboys in high-heeled boots and broad-brimmed Stetsons strolling or riding horseback through town. Numerous working ranches can still be found just a few miles from the center of the city.

Shortcomings: There were numerous complaints about meals being served five miles away from the motel and the attendees having to be bused both ways. The inconvenient, undesirable location of the motel was noted repeatedly. One veteran of Elderhosteling in Tucson noted an inconsistency in staff organization; she wrote that preparation ranged from good to poor on succeeding visits. "Too many canceled projects and no evening plans."

The much-miffed couple also noted that they had never before participated in a program with 100 attendees. A class of 50 is too large when the acoustics are imperfect and the hearing ability of many students is likewise.

Getting In: The Tucson Elderhostel can accommodate a large group, so admission does not seem to be a problem. No programs are scheduled during the desert summer heat, which on occasion feels like the interior of a blast furnace.

Getting There: Tucson has an international airport, Greyhound and Continental bus terminals, and an Amtrak railroad station. In addition, multilane macadam highways lead in and out of town.

Wild Rose Guest Ranch—Northern Arizona University

Courses of Study: The Taming of the Wild West; Cowboys and Indians

Quality of Instructors: Just adequate; not particularly stimulating, according to my panelists.

Environment: NAU leased this property to run an Elderhostel some twenty-five miles from Flagstaff. The guest ranch is nicely located on the shores of Mormon Lake in a pine forest. The location apparently is the program's greatest asset.

Housing: Most of the rooms at the ranch are doubles with private bath facilities.

Food: "So-so. You wouldn't starve."

Unique Attributes: My reviewers had such negative feelings they could not summon up any attributes to report. But summer 1988 was the first time this program was offered. Perhaps improvements will come with experience.

Shortcomings: The entire program is poorly arranged and designed. Because of the distance from Flagstaff, NAU's main campus, the instructors drive back and forth to the ranch each day over country roads. This lack of continuity causes them to take minimal interest in the program or any of the activities.

Even the environment received a black eye. "The mobile home parks are not too scenic," said one couple.

Getting In: Flagstaff is much in demand as a summer destination, but I doubt that reservations at the guest ranch will be oversubscribed within the next few years.

Getting There: Flagstaff is easily reached by air, Continental Trailways bus, or the Santa Fe Railroad. One would have to rent an automobile for the trip from Flagstaff to the ranch.

California

Idyllwild—Idyllwild School of Music and the Arts (ISOMATA)

Courses of Study: Fitness with Folk Dance; Choral Singing; The Ancient World; Photography; Raku Pottery; Choral Music; History of Greece, Egypt, and Israel

Quality of Instructors: Opinions varied regarding the instruction at ISOMATA. All of my panelists enjoyed the cordial atmosphere and effervescent enthusiasm of the teachers, but their ability to teach was somewhat less admired. "Virginia and Ray (program directors and instructors) are an interesting, charming couple—the greatest," wrote an Idyllwild booster.

Environment: Idyllwild is located in a pine forest on the crest of the San Jacinto Mountains, 110 miles east of Los Angeles. There is a quaint little touristy village nearby; otherwise, the school is isolated. If you love the rich remoteness of the woods or were an avid summer camper as a child, the sights and sounds of Idyllwild are filled with nostalgia.

Housing: Elderhostelers sleep in modern log cabins, some with private and others with shared baths. The cottages are scattered in the woods a short walk from the cafeteria. The main lodge, which is used for all day and evening activities, is a brief climb uphill from the cafeteria. Some of the cabins have very pleasant communal rooms with wood-burning fireplaces, cozy spots for marshmallow roasting, or cocktail-hour nibbling and socializing.

Food: The cafeteria is also reminiscent of summer camp. Plain, well-prepared food is served. "When staff were short-handed our Elderhostelers pitched in with the cooking and serving."

Unique Attributes: The folk singing and dancing attract an informal, fun-loving crowd. Because the site is so self-contained, Elderhostelers must, for the most part, create their own evening entertainment.

The mile-high, secluded location tends to make the weather unpredictable. "A late winter snowstorm blanketed the site with soft whiteness and buried the man-made paths and footprints," reported one couple. "It was breathtakingly beautiful." Another couple found themselves at Idyllwild one February during six days of rain. Even though their ardor was dampened, would-be artists and photographers made pictures of raindrops, and they loved it so much they returned the following year. Try to schedule your visit while students are in attendance, too. Some fortunate Elderhostelers were treated to piano performances, vocal concerts, and a dance recital at this residential arts academy.

Shortcomings: The road up the mountain from Palm Springs is hairy; there are few, if any, guardrails and many sharp switchbacks. It is not for the timid, especially in the winter. A less treacherous, longer alternate route is available up the mountain. If you are driving alone, make inquiries first. Bring your boots, earmuffs, and rain gear. The hills are steep between cafeteria, lodge, and cabins.

Getting In: No problems reported, although this program received enthusiastic hurrahs.

Getting There: No public transportation is available to this lovely secluded site.

Los Angeles—University of Judaism

Courses of Study: Jewish Philosophers; Three Jewish Denominations: Biblical Archaeology; Development of Anti-Semitism; Kabbalah and Mysticism; The Prophets

Quality of Instructors: Varying degrees of skill. Several brilliant rabbis, a museum curator, and other less competent instructors teach the Elderhostel program.

Environment: The university, which has a student body of just 201, has a metropolitan setting on a hillside on Mulholland Drive with a beautiful view of the San Fernando Valley. It sits in an exclusive westside residential neighborhood of Los Angeles with access to all the city pleasures.

Housing: The dormitories are luxurious and air-conditioned. Most rooms have private baths. "The new twin-bedded dormitories are the best Elderhostel accommodations I've experienced," wrote one veteran.

Food: I was unable to obtain a consensus regarding the food served. Some comments were: "The dining atmosphere and food are tops." "The well-stocked salad bar is great for dieters!" "Among the best of all my years of Elderhosteling." However, an experienced couple who had attended fourteen Elderhostels said, "The need to serve kosher food strains the budget of the kitchen managers and therefore the menu is limited."

Unique Attributes: The University of Judaism provides a superb cultural and religious experience with thought-provoking programs. The school is a scholarly oasis in the middle of a city of fancy cars, movie stars, and mansions. Elderhostelers can enjoy the special treats of Los Angeles: Chinatown, Japanese sushi bars in Little Tokyo, Universal Studios, and the fantasy of Disneyland. The Elderhostel staff is very warm and helpful.

Shortcomings: Los Angeles has terrible smog, and one has to risk life and limb on the crowded freeways to go anywhere. Both the smog and the traffic can be unnerving experiences for out-of-towners. But there are long waiting lists. One veteran felt "the atmosphere in this program is not conducive to getting to know other Elderhostelers." This was echoed by another couple who said that "groups of fifty Elderhostelers at one time are too large for friendly interaction."

Getting In: These are very popular programs given in a favorite destination, so classes fill up fast. "Always oversubscribed," wrote one Elderhosteler. "We had to

wait two years before getting accepted on the third try."
"We were sixty-fifth on the waiting list but kept trying," wrote another would-be student. The University
of Judaism is frequently filled by lottery (described in
the introduction), even though it has the capacity to
house ninety Elderhostelers at one time.

Getting There: Los Angeles is a city easily reached by
all forms of public transportation. The train to the
West Coast is a superliner with a glass-enclosed,
double-decker observation car. Call 1-800-USA-RAIL
for reservations—and remember to ask for your senior
citizen discount.

Quincy—Feather River College

Courses of Study: Sierra Nevada Wildlife; Flora of
the Sierra; Natural History: Birds; Gentle Wilderness

Quality of Instructors: A caring group of naturalists
and ornithologists lead the field trips and make the
classroom presentations.

Environment: The location in the High Sierras is
spectacular. The area is rich with a heritage of gold
mining and timbering. The nearest town is Quincy, a
village of just 6,000 people. This program is designed
for Elderhostelers seeking an escape into the hushed
beauty of the mountains.

Housing: Elderhostelers are housed in private
apartments.

Food: A nice variety of nutritious meals is served.

Unique Attributes: If you are interested in bird-watching or identifying wild flora and fauna, then this is the place for you. One hosteler wrote, "162 species of birds should intrigue any bird fancier." Hostelers receive lots of tender loving care and go on many bus trips. Feather River is a bird paradise. This hostel provides physical rather than mental stimulation. The college has tennis courts and jogging trails for athletically inclined attendees.

Shortcomings: There is no public transportation to Quincy. It can only be reached by private car.

Getting In: No problems reported.

Getting There: Feather River can only be reached by car, as noted above.

San Clemente—San Clemente Youth Hostel

Courses of Study: Whales; Coastal Wetlands: Birds and Mammal Life; Creative Expression; Yoga; Estuary Wildlife; Stargazing

Quality of Instructors: Energetic, enthusiastic young people with affection for the land, the oceans, and all the wildlife found therein. "Expert outdoor educators."

Environment: This Elderhostel program is held in an International Youth Hostel with a very informal atmosphere. Lots of backpacking youngsters coming and going make this environment lively and interesting for Elderhostelers eager to swap stories with the young hostelers. San Clemente is a charming southern California town that lies halfway between Los Angeles and San Diego on the Pacific Coast.

Housing: Separate men's and women's dormitories with bunk beds and communal baths. Dormitories hold twenty-plus men and women. "Not for light sleepers."

Food: Judged to be satisfactory to excellent. Elderhostelers help with the cleanup.

Unique Attributes: All of the young staff are very agreeable and helpful.

With a car, one can visit either San Diego or Los Angeles, both of which have innumerable attractions. The San Clemente library and beach are within walking distance of the youth hostel.

This program is not designed for Elderhostelers searching for fancy furnishings and slick service, but serious birders and whale watchers should find plenty of memorable experiences. Don't forget to bring your binoculars!

Shortcomings: "The sleeping quarters are noisy and not too much fun, and Elderhostelers are bused to their class locations."

Getting In: No difficulty.

Getting There: The preferred method of enjoying the California coast is by private automobile, but both San Diego and Los Angeles are easily accessible by public transportation.

San Diego—University of California San Diego

Courses of Study: Borderland subjects

Quality of Instructors: Fair

Environment: The city of San Diego sits between forested hills and the Pacific Ocean. It has many tourist attractions, a zoo, an aquarium, and Sea World. San Diego Bay is an important port, and its harbor is full of shore installations of the U.S. Navy. The city's lovely beach area and marina are renowned. The school, however, is located some distance from the beach and marina in an unattractive industrial area. The climate is balmy year-round.

Housing: The dormitory rooms are OK, but one Elderhosteler complained that "the bedding was atrocious and the community rooms were in poor, dilapidated condition."

Food: Meals are good college cafeteria style.

Unique Attributes: San Diego is situated just across the Mexican border from the booming town of Tijuana and offers an unusual opportunity for Elderhostelers to learn about the problems of maintaining social, economic, and political harmony between our two countries. The specific problems of undocumented workers slipping through the "Tortilla Curtain" and the evils of drug traffickers are better understood after program field trips. The San Diego Zoo and Wild Animal Farm contain rare animals and plants displayed in a spectacular natural setting of ravines and canyons. One reviewer noted, "A sincere effort was made to attract some minority Elderhostelers to the program in San Diego. The administration deserves congratulations for its effort."

Shortcomings: This school has not had many years experience hosting Elderhostels; therefore, one of my panelists reviewed the San Diego program charitably. She hoped it will improve its rectifiable weaknesses, such as making better use of the school's advantageous proximity to Tijuana, Mexico. The dormitories are some distance from the food service—not an easy walk for some Elderhostelers.

Getting In: No problems reported.

Getting There: San Diego can be reached by bus, airplane, or major railroad, but an automobile is essential during your stay because of the remote location of the campus. If you rent an automobile, do not forget to ask for your senior citizen perks.

San Francisco—San Francisco International Youth Hostel

Courses of Study: The Many Faces of San Francisco

Quality of Instructors: A very gracious and helpful couple direct the program and serve as hosts and tour guides.

Environment: The hostel is in an excellent location for "doing" San Francisco and listening to the foghorns moan. It is within walking distance of Fisherman's Wharf and Ghirardelli Square and convenient for riding cable cars. The hostel is in a national park overlooking the bay and is served by public buses that have a network of routes all over the city.

Housing: Staying in a youth hostel is neither comfortable nor desirable for seniors. The hostel has bunk beds (lower bunks for seniors) and no closets. Some seniors have to share rooms with young people who are coming and going night and day. The bunk rooms sleep ten or twelve and communal bathrooms are available.

Food: Elderhostelers have meals catered just for them. The food received a rating of very good.

Unique Attributes: The program is well managed and executed. The couple in charge pay careful attention to the needs of all their Elderhostelers. They make arrangements for many day and night trips, purchase matinee tickets when requested, and see to it that no one need go out unaccompanied in the evening. A ten-minute daily chore in the hostel is required of all attendees. International youth hostelers use the facilities, and dialogue with the young people can be very rewarding. "A walking tour of San Francisco is as exciting as walking in Paris."

Shortcomings: The lack of closets or clothes-hanging space can be a disadvantage, especially for women who pack city sight-seeing wardrobes.

Getting In: No problem reported.

Getting There: San Francisco is easily accessible on all forms of public transportation. The city is one of the stops on Amtrak's glass-domed Superchief.

Santa Barbara—Mount St. Mary's College

Courses of Study: May I Introduce You to Yourself; History of the California Missions; Communicating for Success

Quality of Instructors: The sisters and priests of St. Joseph of Carondolet teach very fine classes.

Environment: The Elderhostel program is held at the Franciscan Renewal Center, adjacent to the Old Spanish Mission of Santa Barbara. The center is located just three miles from the Pacific Ocean. The town of Santa Barbara is spread along the Pacific Coast in an area known as the California Riviera. It is situated 100 miles northwest of Los Angeles on one of the most scenic oceanfront drives in the United States. This freeway—the Pacific Coast Highway—winds along the shore, overlooking spectacular sheer cliffs and rock formations. Despite the large University of California campus there, Santa Barbara does not have a particularly intellectual atmosphere. Suntanned students in shorts loll on the beach and toss Frisbees in the air, while luxurious yachts sparkle in the yacht basin.

Housing: Elderhostelers are given nice simple rooms with communal baths down the hall and central showers.

Food: Good plain fare is served.

Unique Attributes: The mission of Santa Barbara, sometimes called the "Queen of the Missions," is famous for its twin towers. The brothers conduct tours of the facility. Santa Barbara is a favorite southern California resort town with miles of beaches on its south-facing shore. The town sits between the cobalt blue Pacific Ocean and a range of purple mountains. The town has preserved its Spanish heritage with distinctively Mediterranean architecture. Red tile roofs cover stucco storefronts and costly mansions are secluded in the mountains, with just their red rooftops peeking through the trees. One reviewer wrote, "A car is not necessary to enjoy this program. Public transportation is readily available to many local scenic and historic sights."

Shortcomings: None reported.

Getting In: In spite of Santa Barbara's proximity to Los Angeles, the program does not seem to be oversubscribed.

Getting There: Santa Barbara can be reached by all forms of public transportation, although a private car is recommended if one wishes to enjoy the scenic splendors of the oceanfront drive. Santa Barbara has a very busy international airport with frequent service from all parts of the country.

Yosemite National Park—Yosemite Institute

Courses of Study: Environmental Education; Flora and Fauna of Yosemite; Natural History of Yosemite National Park

Quality of Instructors: An expert group of naturalists introduce Elderhostelers to the pleasures of enjoying without destroying.

Environment: Twelve hundred square miles of breathtaking beauty comprise Yosemite National Park, situated 200 miles east of San Francisco. "Beautiful! Can't be beat!" said one attendee. Go in the spring to enjoy the torrential, crystal-clear waterfalls, or the grandiose mountains with mammoth peaks and pinnacles, including El Capitan, the largest single block of granite on earth.

Housing: In June, the accommodations are somewhat rugged—wooden, canvas-framed, unheated cabins (twin-bedded, no singles) with rest rooms and shower houses nearby. One can reserve rooms with private baths at the lodge for a small extra charge. In July and August, Elderhostelers stay sixteen miles away in

Extra member of art class, Yosemite Institute, Yosemite, California. (Photo by Mary E. Helfrich)

rough bunkhouses, where mattresses but no linens are supplied. In September, however, Elderhostelers are housed in wooden, heated cabins. These also have rest rooms and showers nearby. Elderhostelers help clean the kitchen, bunkhouse, and bathhouse.

Food: Excellent food is served in the Yosemite Lodge cafeteria, breakfast and dinner only. Lunch is eaten in the field on day-long hikes.

Unique Attributes: Elderhostelers go on all-day hikes on which they learn to tread gently, observe carefully, and listen intently. Some of the highlights of the program are visits to the Mariposa Grove of giant sequoias, dinner at the elegant Awahnee Hotel (extra cost), and viewing the soaring domes of granite and listening to the thunderous sound of the waterfalls. Photo opportunities are provided along the way. Evening programs address conservation topics and management of our national parks.

Shortcomings: This program is designed for the outdoor hosteler, and participants must be in good physical condition. The hikes range from easy to moderate. Rain and snow arrive late in October, and the weather in the park can be very capricious. It can get pretty muddy near the cabins, so protective footwear is recommended. One reviewer wrote, "Tent city is noisy at night, but hopefully, after hiking all day, you will sleep anyway."

Getting In: No problem reported.

Getting There: Take the dramatic automobile drive over one of the four roads that lead into the park. It is possible to get a public bus in Merced, California, which goes to Yosemite.

Colorado

Boulder—University of Colorado

Courses of Study: A broad variety of courses is offered with emphasis on a summer Shakespeare Festival.

Quality of Instructors: The faculty are very good. "Everyone was a pleasure to listen to."

Environment: The university sits right in the middle of a large university town. With an enrollment of almost 23,000 students, it has become one of the leading educational and scientific research centers in the Rocky Mountain states. Boulder is just twenty-five miles north of Denver, and the thousands of acres of campus nestle at the foot of majestic mountains. The area provides excellent skiing and hiking trails for a very health-conscious crowd of students.

Housing: Elderhostelers live in comfortable, high-rise dormitories . The architecture is Italian country villa-style with red-tile roofs.

Food: An excellent variety of college cafeteria meals is served.

Unique Attributes: The University of Colorado provides an ideal combination—a real college environment in a nonurban setting with outstanding faculty and 325 days of sunshine a year. The recreational facilities are exceptional, because the student body is big on recreation. The paths are alive with joggers and bicyclists. Boulder is a town of great scenic beauty. The Continental Divide zigzags north to south through the entire Rocky Mountain range. In the fall the aspens are a fiery blaze of yellow and orange, and the weather is ideal—sunny and temperate with low humidity. The University of Colorado has a museum that houses a splendid and comprehensive dinosaur exhibition.

Shortcomings: No complaints about this program were registered by the Elderhostelers.

Getting In: Apparently, the University of Colorado has been able to register all of the Elderhostelers without long waiting lists.

Getting There: All forms of transportation are available to Denver, and Boulder is served by excellent bus service from Denver.

Colorado Springs—La Foret

Courses of Study: Wildflowers of the Pike's Peak Area; Birds and Songbirds of the Rockies; Conserving the Forest Resources; Outdoor Photography

Quality of Instructors: A team of caring, socially responsible specialists do a very good job of teaching the courses.

Square dancing in Colorado Springs, Colorado. (Photo by Bill Behrends)

Photographing wildflowers in the Rockies, La Foret, Colorado. (Photo by Bill Behrends)

Environment: La Foret is a lovely facility in the Black Forest of Colorado which was built in the 1920s. It is a serene, rustic campsite surrounded by towering blue spruce trees. All of the buildings afford a spectacular view of the reddish granite of Pike's Peak, Colorado's most famous snow-topped mountain. The peak towers 14,110 feet above sea level, but the Ponderosa Lodge and other buildings at La Foret are at an altitude of 7,500 feet. The air in the mountains is dry, crisp, and invigorating.

Housing: Elderhostelers are housed in comfortable four-bedroom, two-bath, one-story cabins. The cottages have central rooms with fireplaces and are heated.

Food: Good meals are served in the modern dining lodge.

Unique Attributes: Delightful side trips are arranged to the Garden of the Gods and Air Force Academy. The Garden of the Gods is a fantastic wilderness park of strangely shaped red rocks sitting amid gnarled junipers. La Foret attracts hostelers who enjoy searching for the delicate beauty of columbines and larkspur and identifying the sounds of obscure bird species. Expect to have many evening discussions about preserving our natural environment.

Shortcomings: La Foret is best reached by private car.

Getting In: No problems reported.

Getting There: The drive from Denver to Colorado Springs enables one to taste and see the best of Colorado's summits. Continental Trailways buses stop in Colorado Springs; Peterson Field accommodates regularly scheduled airlines; in addition, there is an interstate railroad depot.

Durango—Sonlight Christian Camp

Courses of Study: Local Culture; Literature of the Southwest; Geology of Colorado's 14,000-foot Peaks; Narrow Gauge Railroads of the Past

Quality of Instructors: One reviewer reported two out of three instructors were outstanding.

Environment: The camp is located a short distance from town in the San Juan Mountains, sixty miles east of Durango. Durango is a natural gateway to one of the most scenic sections of Colorado, one that includes pre-historic ruins. The town was originally settled by Spanish prospectors, then became a mining and smelting center, but is now a mecca for summer tourists. The San Juan Mountains have jagged, white-topped peaks and almost vertical cliffsides.

Housing: Elderhostelers sleep in modern log facilities that have open, multi-bed dormitories. The accommodations are upstairs and are carpeted. There are communal toilets and showers.

Food: Nice, home-cooked meals are served and there is a weekly cookout.

Unique Attributes: The informal atmosphere at this hostel is very congenial. Interesting side trips are arranged and evening activities planned. Temperatures in and around Durango have been known to plummet from comfortable day temperatures in the seventies to near freezing at night. Remember to bring proper attire. "Hikers in our group claim to have spotted deer on the trail and golden eagles overhead." Some special Colorado wildflowers are the Indian paintbrush, red and blue columbines, and wild geraniums. Evenings are spent debating the beautiful vs. the useful.

Shortcomings: To make the most of the experience, one needs a private car. With a car, one can visit Indian reservations to the south and Mesa Verde National Park with its ancient cliff dwellings thirty-six miles to the west. Visits to the cliff dwellings require a strenuous climb, and the very high elevations (up to 8,500 feet) may adversely affect some persons.

Getting In: No problem reported.

Getting There: Durango can best be reached by private car, but it does have a small airport serviced by America West airlines and several other commuter airlines. The Trailways bus company also serves Durango.

Old Keystone Village—Keystone Science School

Courses of Study: Cross-Country Skiing; Survival in Winter; Aspens in Autumn

Quality of Instructors: Excellent natural science and skiing instructors minister to the needs of the Elderhostelers.

Environment: Keystone Village is situated in a picturesque mountain valley at an elevation of 9,200 feet. The historic old village lies seventy-five miles west of Denver and is an 1880s mining town in the Arapaho National Forest. Keystone Resort is one of Colorado's leading ski areas, with a gondola, nine chair lifts, night skiing and après-ski amenities. The U.S. Ski Team trains on the North Peak of Keystone Mountain. In Colorado's high summits the air is dry and invigorating.

Housing: The sleeping accommodations are rustic log cabins that house five to eight men or women. Wood heat is provided when needed. My panelist found the housing unsatisfactory. She wrote, "Four to a room with one bathroom down the road to be used by ten or more individuals was very poor." It was necessary for Elderhostelers to bring their own linens and sleeping bags, but I understand linens and towels are now provided on request.

Food: Very good, satisfying meals are served in the dining/meeting hall. Participants must assist in meal cleanup.

Unique Attributes: Excellent lessons are provided with splendid opportunities for cross-country skiing and snow-shoeing. Participants build a survival snow house. Cross-country skiing is very strenuous, but the technique is easy to master. In the Rockies, cross-country skiing is particularly rugged because of the mountainous terrain and altitude.

Sharing ski lessons and close sleeping quarters can force sudden friendliness onto a group of strangers. This program is for Elderhostelers who are in excellent physical condition and willing to accept rough and rugged, not-so-posh accommodations. This one is for the "top of the mountain" (not the "over the hill") crowd.

Shortcomings: My reviewers said their only complaint was the poor accommodations. We have been told that new facilities are under construction. Check the status of the new lodge before you register. Remember that cold weather can be stressful.

Getting In: No problems reported.

Getting There: Keystone is best approached by private automobile, but public transportation by bus, train, and chauffered van from Denver's Stapleton Airport are also possible. Old Keystone is situated seventy-five miles west of Denver.

Connecticut

Fairfield—Fairfield University

Courses of Study: Communications; Socrates; Development of Cinema; Native American Art; Economics of the Eighties; Bach's Brandenburg Concertos

Quality of Instructors: An excellent, caring group of professors.

Environment: Fairfield University is located in a pleasant suburban town just one hour on the train from New York City. Fairfield has the élan of extraordinary affluence and is a bedroom community that is as much a New York suburb as it is a Connecticut one. The setting is charming and relaxed with rolling, wooded hills and sweeping lawns. The town is just ten minutes away from the beautiful marinas and beaches of Long Island Sound.

Housing: In general, the housing for the Elderhostel program is very comfortable. The communal dormitories built around a quad tend to be noisy when students are in residence. Single rooms are available with the payment of a single supplement.

Food: The meals are very good.

Unique Attributes: Fairfield's proximity to New York City makes its programs particularly attractive to Elderhostelers who wish to spend some time sightseeing in the city before or after their week at the university. Fairfield is a Catholic university in the Jesuit tradition and boasts a pretty campus that overlooks Long Island Sound.

The physical plant is exceptional; it includes an Olympic-size swimming pool with whirlpool and an inviting lounge area, which is very conducive to pleasant socializing after classes.

Shortcomings: The dormitories are quite a distance from the dining room and classrooms—nice for a walker but a bit much for the not-so-athletic.

Getting In: No problems reported, although this school is a favorite of several much-traveled Elderhostelers who reside on the East Coast.

Getting There: Fairfield is easily reached by suburban train out of Grand Central Station in New York City. It is also served by public buses that one can board in the Manhattan bus terminal.

New London—Connecticut College

Courses of Study: Poetry and Science; Bach's Brandenburg Concertos; Eugene O'Neill's 100th Birthday

Quality of Instructors: An excellent faculty offers an intellectual adventure.

Environment: Connecticut College is located in the city outskirts on a very pretty campus overlooking the eastern entrance of Long Island Sound at the mouth of the Thames River. The college is a small, intimate school with only sixteen hundred students. New London is just a short hop away from Rhode Island, which makes it an ideal starting place for an automobile tour of New England.

Housing: Elderhostelers are housed in adequate single dormitory rooms.

Food: Although there is no choice of main course, the meals are rated as good to OK. The kitchen staff are particularly helpful in adjusting the menu to the needs of special diets.

Unique Attributes: Connecticut's program is well managed by the director. She schedules a few enjoyable extracurricular activities, such as a concert in the campus chapel, a boat ride on the Thames, and square dancing. The college has a superior swimming pool with open swim periods convenient for the hostelers. With an automobile, one can visit an aquarium, arboretum, and art museum as well as stroll the decks of restored tall ships and great whaleships at the Mystic Seaport Museum. New London is also the home of the U.S. Coast Guard Academy and a U.S. submarine base.

Shortcomings: The only complaints I received were from a hypercritical couple who requested ice machines on every floor of the dormitory—a nice touch, but hardly a necessary amenity in college dormitories!

Getting In: The Connecticut College program is very popular because of New London's location on the coast midway between the eastern metropolises of Boston and New York. Early registration is absolutely necessary.

Getting There: New London can be reached by all forms of public transportation as well as private automobile over a network of superhighways.

West Hartford—St. Joseph's College for Women

Courses of Study: Herbs; Genealogy: A Look at Your Family Tree; Louis XIV Court; Lifestyles of the Rich and Famous; Victorian Art and Architecture

Quality of Instructors: All of the college professors received an excellent rating.

Environment: St. Joseph's College has a quiet, green, landscaped campus with lots of trees and a lovely relaxed atmosphere. West Hartford, an upscale suburb of the city of Hartford, combines the pleasures of urban and suburban living.

Housing: The dormitories are typical college dorms with communal bathrooms down the hall, but St. Joseph's dorms are "white glove" clean. Single rooms are available if desired.

Food: The meals are very good. A sincere effort is made to please the guests and to serve a healthful array of foods.

Unique Attributes: The geographic location of West Hartford seems to be St. Joseph's primary draw. Some of my reviewers wrote about sightseeing through Connecticut on the way to school, then continuing to other Elderhostels in New England. Other panelists described trips to Tanglewood, the summer home of the Boston Symphony Orchestra and the Jacob's Pillow dance festival.

Unlike many Elderhostel institutions, St. Joseph's permits registration for two consecutive weeks, an ideal arrangement if one wishes to tour the Berkshires during the mid-session weekend. Drive north on Route 91 to explore the Connecticut River Valley or head west to the Lee/Lenox area for wonderful music and summer theater.

Shortcomings: In the official Elderhostel catalog, St. Joseph's brags about its rave reviews. I did receive positive feedback as noted above, but I also heard that the lack of air-conditioning in the dormitories can be a serious nuisance in July. Also the room air-conditioners in the classrooms work only erratically, and the evening scheduled programs only rated a fair.

"Tell the folks they'd better bring their own fans!" one of my contributors wrote.

Getting In: No problems reported.

Getting There: One has plenty of choices of transportation to Hartford. Wings to the Springfield/Hartford airport, and wheels and motor coach to the college are available, although your own wheels are preferable.

Florida

Brooksville—University of Southern Florida, Chinsegut Hill

Courses of Study: Thomas Jefferson; Government in the Shadows; Why Dig Holes in the Ground?; Franklin and the Early Republic

Quality of Instructors: "Top notch," according to the reviewers. All the university professors are scholarly and present the material in an interesting fashion.

Environment: The Elderhostel program is held at an educational conference center, a research center of the U.S. Department of Agriculture, pleasantly located fifty-five miles north of Tampa near the Gulf of Mexico. The center sits in a green forest in the Florida Uplands, a region that is only 200 to 300 feet above sea level, but breezes from the Gulf relieve the summer heat.

Housing: Elderhostelers are housed in four-bedroom, two-bath cabins that are very clean, comfortable, and air-conditioned.

Food: The meals, served in the multipurpose center, are very good.

Unique Attributes: The climate on the Gulf Coast of Florida is less humid than the Atlantic Coast, and the elevation is higher. This facility is a Department of Agriculture cattle-breeding station and the main building, the Manor House, is an 1842 historic dwelling. The classroom facility used for the Elderhostel program is new and comfortable. Tampa is a cigar-making and shipbuilding center, although tourism is the major industry of the state.

Shortcomings: The humidity in Florida can be brutal in the summer, with or without breezes from the Gulf.

Getting In: All Elderhostel programs in Florida are popular during the winter months. Early registration is recommended.

Getting There: The Brooksville program can be reached by either wheels or wings. Bus, plane, and train go to Tampa, but Brooksville does not have an airport.

Georgia

Atlanta—Simpsonwood Conference and Retreat Center

Courses of Study: Civil War and the Battle of Atlanta; Astronomy and God's Creation; Indians in Georgia

Quality of Instructors: The Elderhostel teachers are very serious educators.

Environment: The conference center is located ten miles from Atlanta on 239 acres stretched along the banks of the Chattahoochee River. The atmosphere is "very cool, quiet, and reserved." As a Methodist retreat, it purports to have a reflective, restful ambience. The countryside is gorgeous. In the spring-time, the fragrance of magnolia and dogwood fills the air, and some classic antebellum-period homes can be found on the outskirts of the city. The climate of Georgia is balmy, and the rich, red soil nourishes the cotton fields.

Housing: Elderhostelers stay in a brand-new lodge that is heated and air-conditioned. Each room has a private bath and two double beds. There are no radios or TVs in the building.

Food: Simple fare is prepared by the chef and served in a dining room. An inoffensive nonsectarian blessing precedes each meal. Peaches, peanuts, and pecans are plentiful.

Unique Attributes: Wonderful evening activities are included in the Elderhostel program. Atlanta, Georgia's largest city, has a plethora of performing arts; theater, ballet, and the Atlanta Symphony are among the choices. Elderhostelers are bused to all off-campus activities in an unusually comfortable, air-conditioned motor coach.

Shortcomings: No problems or weaknesses.

Getting In: In spite of its easy access, this program is not usually oversubscribed.

Getting There: The administration of Simpsonwood provides transportation from the Hartsfield International Airport, one of the country's busiest. Arrangements can probably be made for pickup if you arrive by bus or train.

Hawaii

Honolulu—University of Manoa

Courses of Study: The Examined Life (an intensive, two-week course)

Quality of Instructors: The professors are exemplary.

Environment: This Elderhostel program is conducted on a thirty-five-acre campus (covered with a wide variety of exotic plants) on the outskirts of Honolulu. Public bus service runs from the campus to all of the recreational, cultural, and business centers of the metropolitan area. Hawaii, our fiftieth state, is a favorite tourist destination for people on the mainland. The course title, adapted from a well-known Socratic quotation, establishes the solemn, serious mood of this particular Elderhostel.

Housing: The student dormitories are beautiful, round buildings but are poorly maintained. The lack of air-conditioning in the dormitories can test the fortitude of attendees.

Food: My reviewers rate the university cafeteria as just fair.

Unique Attributes: Abe Arkoff, a consulting psychologist who has taught many years as a teacher, trainer, and counselor, leads this very special workshop. Abe, a humanist in the school of Rogers and Maslow, has been in hospice work for seven years, and his insights about dying are from firsthand observation. Participants are taught to face their own deaths with nobility by examining their lives and finishing any unresolved business. Making a will is just one step in clearing the past. Participants are guided through an eleven-point "Dying Readiness" test, because experience shows that the easiest deaths are had by those who have examined their lives and cleared their pasts.

If the course is well received, plans are being formulated to add a winter seminar on the same subject on Waikiki. Elderhostelers are treated to afternoon educational tours of Oahu and evening Hawaiian cultural events.

Shortcomings: The summer temperatures in Hawaii range between 85 and 93 degrees. One reviewer, a native New Englander, found the humidity oppressive. She may have encountered what the native islanders call "Kona weather," when the trade winds forget to blow. She was distressed by the lack of air-conditioning on the tour buses.

Getting In: All of the attendees reported this as their "best" Elderhostel experience; however, they also wrote that initially the course was canceled for lack of sufficient interest. Not yet a popular program.

Getting There: Hawaii can be reached by all major airlines or on a leisurely cruise ship from Los Angeles or San Francisco.

Honolulu, Island of Oahu—University of Hawaii at Honolulu

Courses of Study: Journal Keeping

Quality of Instructors: This course is taught by a caring, dedicated man who is willing to share his own methods of problem-solving with the class.

Environment: The native Hawaiian population is a fascinating mix of Polynesian, Chinese, Japanese, Caucasian, and Filipino. The city of Honolulu is also an uncommon mix of concrete and coral bordered with sand and coco palm trees. On the nearby beach of Waikiki, the cheek-to-jowl towers of the commercial hotels obliterate many views of the ocean; but the weather is perfect most of the year. Brief tropical storms can be expected in January and February.

Housing: The accommodations are adequate except for visitations from an unendangered species—the cockroach! "If squeamish about insects, you'd better stay home."

Food: My reviewers found the food too institutional, but if you are mad about macadamias, the nuts are much less expensive on the island than on the mainland.

Unique Attributes: This course covers journal keeping not as a literary masterpiece but as a vehicle for writing through one's problems. This Elderhostel offers one the opportunity to stay on after the program to loll on the beach of Waikiki or combine it with another hostel back-to-back. The most beautiful, unspoiled part of Hawaii are the outer islands. The volcanic islands of Kaui, Maui, Molokai, and the big island of Hawaii are not yet crowded with hotels and tourists. One can still find plantations of sugar cane and pineapple fields. Heavy rainfall (annual precipitation is over 400 inches on Kauai) makes the vegetation unbelievably lush. The Honolulu anthurium nursery is a not-to-be-missed wonder. Displayed are seventeen hundred varieties of orchids—pink, purple, green, yellow, and striped.

Shortcomings: The expensive cost of flying to Hawaii limits the number of Elderhostelers able to enjoy this program.

Getting There: Most major cities in the United States have nonstop jet service to Honolulu.

Oahu—Brigham Young

Courses of Study: Oceanography; Volcanoes; Polynesian Culture; Medicinal Use of Native Plants

Quality of Instructors: The teachers are very good, and interaction with the students is encouraged and very pleasant.

Environment: Hawaii is the only one of our United States with a truly oriental flavor. The campus is located amid the tropical beaches and majestic mountains of Oahu. The school is located right next to the Polynesian Culture Center, where there are many exhibits of carved figures of Hawaiian gods and other sacred spirits.

Housing: The accommodations are fine.

Food: An amazing variety of attractively prepared fresh fruits and vegetables is offered.

Unique Attributes: Field trips for on-site learning are well designed and organized. Elderhostelers participate in an authentic Polynesian luau, a Hawaiian show and buffet, and visit the orchid garden.

Shortcomings: None reported.

Getting In: Hawaiian programs are not heavily subscribed because of the cost of getting there.

Getting There: Most major airlines serve the Hawaiian Islands.

Idaho

Rexburg—Ricks College

Courses of Study: Fire Opals of Idaho; The Teton Dam Disaster; Color Slide Photography

Quality of Instructors: Instructors are unusually knowledgeable, helpful, and pleasant. '

Environment: Rexburg is a clean, attractive small town in Idaho's historic Snake River Valley, an area founded by fur traders and gold miners. Yellowstone National Park and the snowy peaks of the Grand Tetons are just ninety miles away across the border in Wyoming. The valley lies in a white pine forest, its roads bordered with handsome bushes of mock orange and views of the Snake River twisting through the woods.

Housing: Elderhostelers are housed in very modern student apartments that contain two bedrooms, a bath, sitting room, and kitchen. The apartment complex also has laundry facilities.

Food: Meals are reported to be plentiful and tasty with a good variety of choices.

Unique Attributes: Ricks College is a two-year school run by the Mormon Church. Certain standards of dress and conduct are expected of everyone on campus. Smoking and drinking of alcohol are prohibited—even coffee and tea are not served. A variety of evening activities is available on this beautiful campus, including swimming, bowling, and music concerts. The distances between buildings are convenient and comfortable for walking. Field trips take Elderhostelers along quiet paths away from the tourist routes to search out hot springs and geysers. These are laboratory courses that require the use of equipment and instruments.

Shortcomings: No weaknesses reported.

Getting In: Idaho is not a particularly popular vacation destination, but the Ricks College course frequently has waiting lists. One of my reviewing couples was accepted from a waiting list. The course has a total capacity of thirty or forty students, but one may have to share laboratory equipment in the classroom.

Getting There: Ricks College can be reached by bus or plane, but private automobile permits extra sightseeing while driving to and from the campus.

Iowa

Iowa City—University of Iowa

Courses of Study: Two-week intensive workshops in the writing of short fiction or poetry.

Quality of Instructors: Three members of the famous Writers' Workshop are selected each summer to work in the Elderhostel program. Most literary critics believe these young graduate students to be the cream of the crop. All of the instructors are knowledgeable and supportive.

Environment: The small-town college atmosphere is almost perfect. The Iowa River flows leisurely through the 1,880-acre campus with buildings on both shores connected by charming footbridges. "It's River City from *The Music Man.*" Students can be seen paddling canoes along the river and families of noisy ducks provide a pleasant diversion while you walk to and from classes. The campus architecture is a charming mix of old and new buildings, all flanked with broad green lawns.

Housing: Modern dormitories are comfortable and convenient to all campus activities, classrooms, and the cafeteria. Single rooms, typewriters, and small refrigerators are available for a modest additional cost.

Campus along the Iowa River, University of Iowa, Iowa City, Iowa. (Photo by Mary E. Helfrich)

Union footbridge, University of Iowa.

Student and teacher, University of Iowa.

Try to get a river view if you can. All rooms have individual air-conditioning units and the buildings have elevators.

Food: The cafeteria menus have too many temptations for calorie-counters, but nutritious selections are also available. "Watch it! Food is excellent and overeating comes easy!" one reviewer wrote. "They even fixed grits for me!" The cafeteria is a large, friendly, noisy dining area, and its round tables encourage Elderhostelers to have leisurely conversations with students of this large, diverse campus body.

Unique Attributes: This is not a laid-back, get-a-little-local-culture hostel. For the most part, participants are serious writers or would-be writers.

Waiting for the van, University of Iowa.

Stanley Residence Hall, University of Iowa.

Course includes heavy reading and writing assignments, and small classes of peers critique one another's work. One invaluable program component is one-on-one student-teacher conferences scheduled once or twice during each workshop. The annual publication of a book of short stories and poetry written by workshop attendees is the frosting on the cake.

Peggy Houston, the state Elderhostel coordinator, is "tops." She plans for participants to enjoy all the university offerings at no additional cost: good theater, symphony concerts, and weekend day trips. She also provides daily van service for those attendees who cannot manage the distance to class or other activities.

A four-year veteran wrote, "How lucky we are! I'll continue to reapply each year, because I love the experience, the people I've met, and the personal development. Late-night reading of my own work is one of the unique pleasures that brings me back year after year."

Shortcomings: "I would like a full professor for one of our classes," at least two veterans commented. "Good beds but lousy pillows," another attendee charged.

Getting In: Very early registration is a must. The classes fill to capacity very quickly. If you are frozen out by registering too late—as I was one year—take comfort in knowing that the wait will make the experience all the more rewarding one year later.

Getting There: Iowa City is easily reached by automobile if you like to drive. Cedar Rapids is served by bus and several airlines. The limo driver from Cedar Rapids to Iowa City is a joyful local booster!

Iowa City—University of Iowa

Courses of Study: Intensive four-week writing program in the novel.

Quality of Instructors: Excellent. Teachers are graduates of the Iowa Writers' Workshop, a school that turns out prize-winning American authors.

Environment: Iowa City is a charming university town with tree-shaded streets and mature perennial gardens. It is known as a cultural center—the Athens of the Midwest—with upscale bookstores, trendy boutiques, and plenty of charming college bistros with checkered tablecloths and hanging greenery.

Housing: Students are housed in spacious enough rooms in high-rise dormitories directly across the street from the college cafeteria. The dormitories have individual room air-conditioners and elevators and are ideally situated for strolling to downtown shops, parks, museums, theaters, and indoor swimming pools. This large university has ten dormitories, making it possible for most undergraduates and all Elderhostelers to live in college housing.

Food: Sure it is steam-table cafeteria food, but the quantities are unlimited and the choices almost infinite. Even finicky eaters should manage well here.

Unique Attributes: This program offers an opportunity to spend four weeks with a group of your peers, all of whom are serious about their writing. Walking to class along the banks of the Iowa River or feeding the ducks will stir a writer's imagination, and the livable quality of Iowa City seems to foster the introspection writers need. Comments from reviewers were, "Some suprisingly good writers, may see some of them in hardcover yet!" "An intellectual bargain with a great bunch of people who have lived long enough not to be intimidated by professors." Iowa City has too many irresistible distractions: classic films for movie buffs at the Bijou, science lectures, the Iowa Symphony, a light opera company, and evening readings of the work of resident poets and authors.

Shortcomings: Several reviewers found the four-week session too long and felt that their work was short-changed by the depth of the criticism.

Getting In: The four-week novel writing program is not as heavily oversubscribed as the two-week writing programs.

Getting There: See the previous evaluation of the University of Iowa's two-week programs.

Ottumwa—Indian Hills College

Courses of Study: Ceramics; Archaeology; Watercolor

Quality of Instructors: "Great watercolor artist/ teacher makes everyone feel successful, and the archaeology professor gives excellent lectures on the history of the Iowa Indian tribes!"

Environment: The wooded campus of Indian Hills College, formerly a religious school for women, is beautiful. The carpets of green grass surround lovely little lakes, and the land is not "nearly as flat as we've been led to believe." Ottumwa is in southern Iowa, an area noted for its prime farmland and for its corn, hogs, and soybeans.

Housing: Elderhostelers share college dormitories with a group of very courteous and thoughtful students. Communal bath facilites are down the hall.

Food: "Excellent. No complaints," my panelist responded.

Unique Attributes: "The best of ten Elderhostels attended," wrote my reviewer, a California resident. In addition to enjoying the well-organized and well-planned extracurricular activities and classes, my reviewer found the campus had a charming feeling of uncrowded space and the state of Iowa a surprising sense of sophistication. The advanced music students perform in a concert that exhibits their talent and training. This, too, is charming.

Grant Wood is one of Iowa's most famous native sons. Arrangements are made for the Elderhostel class to have individual photographs taken of themselves standing behind life-size, cardboard-cutout figures of the Grant Wood farmer and his wife, replicated from his painting *American Gothic.*

Shortcomings: Ottumwa is not an easily reached destination.

Getting In: My reviewer made early reservations so she had no difficulty being accepted.

Getting There: The best method of going to Ottumwa is by railroad: the main line going both east and west still stops in Ottumwa.

Archaeology class, Indian Hills College, Ottumwa, Iowa. (Photo by Mary E. Helfrich)

Ceramics class, Indian Hills College, Ottumwa, Iowa. (Photo by Mary E. Helfrich)

Kentucky

Corbin—Otter Creek Park

Courses of Study: Flora, Fauna, and Poetry Writing

Quality of Instructors: Young and enthusiastic naturalists whose ardor and high spirits are contagious.

Environment: The park is a 3,000-acre tract of forest, abandoned farms, and caves adjoining the Ohio River. Elderhostelers can enjoy the solitary space of woods and water and think about preserving the delicate balance of our ecology.

Housing: Elderhostelers stay in modern facilities with private baths, daily maid service, and superb views of the Ohio River.

Food: The meals served in the park restaurant are excellent in both quality and quantity.

Unique Attributes: The park offers great forest and meadow areas for the field study of plants and animals as well as a unique opportunity to watch the barge traffic rolling on the Ohio River. Evenings are filled with special courses and demonstrations such as free-form basket weaving, wool carding, and making dyes of native plant materials. Interesting side trips are arranged to the historic Doe Run Inn and the Gatton Museum of artillery at nearby Fort Knox, the repository of America's gold reserves. The park is only thirty miles from Louisville—home of the Kentucky Derby, the most famous horse race in the United States—and 100 miles from Mammoth Cave, an incredible network of caves and rows of white stalactites that have been explored by speleologists.

Shortcomings: None reported, even though the park has not been offering Elderhostel programs for many years. A private car is needed for transportation.

Getting In: No difficulties reported.

Getting There: Only accessible by private car, although the Louisville Standiford International Airport is served by all major airlines.

Cumberland Falls State Resort Park— Union College

Courses of Study: History of the Area; Music of Appalachia; Study of Trees, Wildlife, and Caves; The Perception of Appalachia through Film

Quality of Instructors: The teachers from the college in Barbourville are very good. The demonstrations of handmade musical instruments and foot-stompin' mountain music are excellent.

Environment: The woodlands of the park glow with beautiful yellow aspens in autumn, and the steep sides of the pass shimmer with the pale pinks of mountain laurel and rhododendrons in the spring. Cumberland Falls is known as "The Niagara of The West." The Cumberland Gap is a natural pass through the Appalachians used by the pioneers going west. Daniel Boone blazed his wilderness trail through the Cumberland Pass. Railroads now run through the pass and it has become the site of a national park.

Housing: DuPont Lodge is a deluxe lodge run by the State of Kentucky. The double rooms are very nice; they have two double beds and private baths.

Food: Excellent food is served in a beautiful dining room overlooking the Cumberland River.

Unique Attributes: Cumberland Falls is renowned for its "moonbow," a beautiful physical phenomenon created by moonlight filtering through the mist of the falls. The park is surrounded by a very depressed area of Appalachia. Elderhostelers can see and hear about the abject poverty and hardships of life in the mountains in addition to discussing the history of corruption and economics of the area.

Some Elderhostel programs include explorations of mysterious and "scary" caves, while other programs have field trips to the site of the famous Scopes trial, where Clarence Darrow and William Jennings Bryan argued the teaching of Darwin's theory of evolution. The park is located a short distance from the Lincoln Museum, a collection of 250,000 objects devoted to the great president. Alumni of Cumberland Falls recommend this program for senior seniors; the hiking, walking, boating, and swimming are all pleasantly accessible.

Shortcomings: Some reviewers believed the class of fifty Elderhostelers too many for an optimum learning experience.

Getting In: Alumni of Cumberland Falls suggest making early reservations.

Getting There: This part of Kentucky has an excellent network of federal highways.

Pleasant Hill—Shaker Village

Courses of Study: The Search for the I Finite

Quality of Instructors: Instructors have an excellent ability to interpret the material for the students.

Environment: The setting is most unusual. It is a 2,250-acre site just twenty-five miles south of Lexington. Elderhostelers live in restored Shaker buildings and study the Shaker beliefs as well as those of other unusual religions, including the myths of the mountain people. The Shaker Village has been designated a national landmark. The mild temperatures of the area of Kentucky near Lexington encourage tobacco farming and the breeding of horses.

Housing: "The best of many Elderhostels I've attended." The rooms with private baths are those used for tourists in season and are furnished with reproductions of classic Shaker furniture.

Food: Elderhostelers are treated to traditional Kentucky food, a very good but unusual style of cooking. "Beaten biscuits and hickory smoked ham!"

Unique Attributes: In Kentucky people still live close to the land, a verity that relates to the subject of the course. The village is a living tribute to the beauty and simplicity of the Shaker culture, and the hands-on experience brings to life the facts, ideas, and forces that shaped these religious tenets. This sect has dwindled to a handful of remaining members who weave their own fabrics and spin wool and live in New England. The society was noted for fine farms, industry and ingenuity. The lovely furniture is now prized as collectors' items.

Shortcomings: None reported.

Getting In: This is a popular destination and as such requires early registration.

Getting There: Lexington is a major airport with direct and connecting flights from all over the United States. Fly in and rent a car, or take your own wheels if you have the time and energy to meander over the back roads of Kentucky.

Maine

Biddeford—University of New England

Courses of Study: Introduction to the Verdi Operas; The Plains Indians; Down East Maine; History of the Southern Maine Coast—Sites and Memorabilia

Quality of Instructors: Varies from excellent to instructors who are not too well prepared.

Environment: The University of New England is a small, independent school located on the Saco River on the outskirts of Biddeford. The school has an enrollment of just 600 career-minded students and a campus spread over 122 acres. Biddeford, with its sandy beaches and sea breezes, sits in the low coastal region on the Atlantic Ocean twenty miles south of Portland and just two hours' drive from Boston. Nearby are the popular holiday seaside resorts of Old Orchard and Kennebunkport.

Housing: Elderhostelers stay in typical college dormitories with shared bath facilities.

Food: The food is excellent: lots of salad, juices, fresh fruit, and wholesome main dishes are served.

Unique Attributes: The Elderhostel leadership is very conscientious.

The new student center has excellent facilities for physical fitness and health. The University of New England has only been in existence since 1978, formed by the consolidation of St. Francis College and the New England College of Osteopathic Medicine. The laid-back atmosphere of Maine encourages creativity. Many artists and writers have established colonies and retreats on the islands and inland lakes, and the ocean-side shopping streets of Biddeford are filled with art galleries and quaint craft shops.

Shortcomings: Several reviewers agreed that the range of subjects taught was too broad, despite which they like meeting Elderhostelers with varied backgrounds and interests.

Getting In: No problems reported.

Getting There: Biddeford can be reached by expressways, interstate buses, or plane to Portland.

Bryant Pond—Maine's Conservation Camp

Courses of Study: Forestry; Flora and Fauna of Environs; Birding

Quality of Instructors: A group of very good, caring experts.

Environment: The camp is located in a bucolic setting on a lovely wooded lake surrounded by tall white pines. Inland Maine is sparsely settled, but all those trees have made the state a leader in paper making and toothpick manufacturing. And look at all those Christmas trees! Winters in Maine are harsh and snowy, but the summers are filled with tourists and with small country fairs and craft shows.

Housing: The accommodations are in rugged cabins with communal baths. My reviewers rated the housing as inadequate. "The rooms are separated by thin partitions rather than walls."

Food: The meals are poor. "Skimpy cuisine served on metal mess kits with no extras and no seconds."

Unique Attributes: The setting is very beautiful and lends itself to the study of nature. Life in rural Maine moves at a slow pace and the laconic Yankees live close to the land. During the drive to Bryant Pond, one journeys through tall pine forests and agricultural areas where the dominant crops are potatoes and blueberries.

Shortcomings: "This camp is not suitable for Elderhostelers. It is run like a Boy Scout camp."

Getting In: No difficulties reported.

Getting There: Accessible only by private car. My panelists suggested avoiding the monotonous interstate highways and following the backcountry roads instead.

Camden—Figaro Sailing Program

Courses of Study: Sailing, Seamanship, and Coastal Studies

Quality of Instructors: Excellent, especially the first mate.

Environment: "Anchors aweigh! The Atlantic Ocean—can't beat it!"

Housing: Aboard a small, fifty-one-foot yawl that accommodates six Elderhostelers and a crew of six. A limited number of single and double berths are on board.

Food: Simple but hearty. Strictly vegetarian vittles are served on shipboard.

Unique Attributes: Elderhostelers live aboard a sailboat and sail to a different island each day after embarking from the picturesque Penobscot Bay harbor. A voyage under sail has a uniquely exhilarating element of risk. Elderhostelers learn sail handling, trimming, anchoring, and coastal navigation. They try beachcombing on uninhabited islands and study the flora and fauna.

This Elderhostel is truly an adventure. It requires skill and endurance to learn how to conquer the winds and currents, battle tides, and steer a course through twisting channels in all kinds of weather. The sea is a strict disciplinarian.

Shortcomings: The quarters are very crowded. If the weather were very cold or wet for an extended period, the close quarters would probably be too confining.

Getting In: No problem.

Getting There: Camden can be reached by bus, plane, or private automobile. Delta Airline flies to Bangor, fifty miles away, and Valley, a commuter line, flies from Boston to Camden.

Portland—Westbrook College

Courses of Study: Masterpieces of French Art; The Piano in Contemporary Music; Science of Human Evolution; Stones and Bones

Quality of Instructors: Very sincere, particularly the concert pianist who performed as well as lectured.

Environment: The campus is located on the quiet, tree-shaded streets of Portland. Portland is a famous old fishing port; its piers abound with craggy-faced fishermen hauling in lobster, clams and cold-water fish. Portland is an oft-used jumping-off place for touring inland Maine and driving up the rockbound coast where one can find busy public beaches abutting pricey waterfront homes. Artists and writers find creative inspiration in the rugged coast and in the spirited individuality of the people.

Housing: Adequate.

Food: College cafeteria style. Lots of wonderful blueberries and fresh fish.

Unique Attributes: The Joan Whitney Payson Gallery on the campus is a little gem of a museum and is used as part of the art class. Portland is a New England city that offers a variety of cultural opportunities; it hosts a resident theater company, an art museum, a symphony orchestra, and a contemporary dance company. The Portland String Quartet is renowned throughout the country. Portland is situated on the coast, an ideal location for relaxing on the pier to watch lobster boats being loaded with traps, to watch the surf break into foam against the reefs, or to admire the skilled shipbuilders, who still build seaworthy vessels by hand.

Shortcomings: None. Westbrook has been offering Elderhostel programs for the past ten years, and the administration has become very proficient.

Getting In: No problems reported.

Getting There: Portland is a major city and is easily reached by plane, train, or interstate bus.

Presque Isle—University of Maine at Presque Isle

Courses of Study: Body Recall (a nonstrenuous, gentle exercise class); Today's Rocks and Yesterday's Fossils; Native Peoples

Quality of Instructors: All of the teachers are excellent; the exercise instructor makes the workout "good fun" and the geology professor is outstanding.

Environment: Presque Isle is located in the northeast corner of Maine in Aroostock County, bordering New Brunswick, Canada. Presque Isle is a small town in the heart of potato farm country. The University of Maine's branch campus, a four-year coed institution for 1,285 undergraduates, is within walking distance of town.

Housing: Elderhostelers stay in two-person dormitory rooms with common bath facilities.

Food: The cafeteria menu is very good, plentiful, and of considerable variety. Breakfast starts with fresh doughnuts every morning, eggs cooked to order, and a cereal bar. Other culinary treats at Presque Isle are an ice-cream machine and a well-stocked dessert bar.

Unique Attributes: The field trips are particularly interesting: the geologic formations; basket weaving at the Micmac Indian reservation and school; the planetarium; and the visit to Grand Falls, New Brunswick. The informal picnics, on the field trips and at a private camp on a north woods lake, tend to create a congenial hostel group. The campus has tennis courts and a renowned old summer playhouse.

Shortcomings: "None that I recall," commented my panelists.

Getting In: "A breeze—it was our first choice."

Getting There: My panelists drove up the coast of Maine, but one could reach Presque Isle by Greyhound or Trailways bus or plane. Delta and Eastern airlines serve Presque Isle.

Waterville—Thomas College

Courses of Study: Indoor Horticulture; Marine Life in the Gulf of Maine; Films; Nuclear Weapons and the Arms Race

Quality of Instructors: The instructors are excellent, and in addition to professors from the college, courses are taught by experts in the various fields. The State Commissioner of Fish and Game offered the students a new way of looking at their physical environment.

Environment: Thomas College offers a serene setting. The landscaped campus for just 832 students is situated on the outskirts of the town along the Kennebec River. Waterville is the entrance to the Belgrade Lakes region, where glistening lakes are surrounded by woodlands filled with dark evergreens and slender white birches.

Housing: Elderhostelers have private rooms and baths in a motellike building.

Food: Very good classic college fare is served in an appetizing fashion.

Unique Attributes: The program is very well organized and operated. The extracurricular events are particularly interesting; hostelers go to theater in the restored 1902 Opera House and visit a Player Piano Museum. Waterville is just an hour's scenic drive west from the rockbound coast through the uninhabited reaches of the state. Maine is the largest of all the New England states, and the distances are extensive between the inland cities. North and west of Waterville one can still find backcountry roads that follow lovely winding rivers .

Shortcomings: No faults were found in Waterville.

Getting In: No problems reported.

Getting There: Waterville has limited plane service through Eastern Express from Boston but very good interstate bus service.

Maryland

Baltimore—Peabody Institute

Courses of Study: Origins of Jazz; Romantic Composers; Walters Art Museum; Bach Lieder Accompaniment; Art of Chamber Music; Genesis of Opera; Beethoven's String Quartets

Quality of Instructors: Because Peabody is a favorite destination for so many Elderhostelers, I received numerous evaluations of this program. Ratings of instructors ranged from superior to first-rate to just fair. One respondent wrote that he had learned from experience that "good musicians are not necessarily good teachers." The music classes are augmented by the use of recordings and the piano, and the museum course is conducted by a docent of exceptional ability.

Environment: Peabody sits right in the middle of Baltimore, a cosmopolitan city that still retains some provincial charm. The architecture of Peabody combines ornate French and English Renaissance. Baltimore has recently been revitalized and given a face-lift. A decrepit harbor has been transformed into a glittering array of boutiques and restaurants. One can even cruise the harbor in a ship. The Aquarium and Walter's Art Gallery, built in the style of an Italian Renaissance palazzo, are two of the big-city treats to be

Statue of Peabody in park facing the school, Baltimore, Maryland. (Photo by Barbara L. Silvers)

Peabody Conservatory of Music, Baltimore, Maryland. (Photo by Barbara L. Silvers)

Peabody Conservatory, Baltimore, Maryland. (Photo by Barbara L. Silvers)

found in Baltimore. The old city still has homes with bright white marble stoops on cobblestone streets.

Housing: Elderhostelers sleep in modern, air-conditioned dormitories. The high-rise, elevator-equipped buildings, which surround a central mall, are adequate. Separate men's and women's lavatory facilities are on the same floor. The bedrooms are good size, and there is a pleasant central lounge.

Food: Typical college fare is served in a student dining room. "It is ordinary college food—not gourmet." A more critical couple, with a great deal of Elderhostel experience, judged the food "poor."

Unique Attributes: Peabody Institute educates intense, dedicated students of music, and the Elderhostelers reflect this serious approach. In the spring, many high-quality recitals are given by graduating students; Elderhostelers are encouraged to attend the concerts, because the students need practice playing before an audience. In addition, concerts and recitals are frequently given by Peabody faculty.

"You are surrounded by music from early morning through bedtime. The sounds of voice and instruments pour from practice rooms constantly, delightfully." "Wall to wall music," enthused another panelist. "For anyone interested in music, this is heaven!"

Peabody is within walking distance of the waterfront redevelopment, restaurants, and recently gentrified areas of the city. Public transportation is convenient and has good schedules.

Shortcomings: Peabody always receives accolades for its program. My sample would indicate that Peabody is as popular on the East Coast as the University of Judaism is on the West. I was told, "There aren't any shortcomings." However, the critical couple found the food not as good as most of the Elderhostels they have attended.

Getting In: Peabody is a very popular destination and usually has waiting lists for the Elderhostel program—particularly in the spring, when student recitals are required by the curriculum. Even with early registration, admission is not assured. Some panelists wrote about long waiting lists.

Getting There: Baltimore is served by all forms of public transportation. Major air carriers, buses, and railroads all have frequent service.

Takoma Park—Columbia Union College

Courses of Study: Dramatics; Astronomy; Historical Survey of Washington, D.C.; Short Stories; Music for Enjoyment; Computer for the User

Quality of Instructors: The college professors at Columbia Union are able and excellent.

Environment: The school is situated just seven miles from Washington, D.C., and offers a wonderful opportunity for students to get to know and see our capital firsthand. Takoma Park is really a bedroom community for Washington.

This college is a church-related school. The Seventh Day Adventists prohibit any smoking or drinking of alcoholic beverages on campus.

Housing: Elderhostelers stay in quite satisfactory student dormitories. The dorms are air-conditioned, and single rooms are available.

Food: Good to excellent. Very tasty vegetarian, with a well-stocked salad bar, delicious casserole dishes, and a frozen yogurt machine. Great home-baked goods, too. Despite the Seventh Day Adventist strictures, coffee is served to the Elderhostelers.

Unique Attributes: This is a small college in a suburban community located right on the Washington metro line, if one wishes to do any additional sightseeing. The program-conducted tours, however, of the Smithsonian, the Capitol, monuments, and memorials are very interesting and enjoyable because of the harmonious group. This is a very conscientiously run program. "The final banquet is as fancy and beautifully set up as any Elderhostel I've attended." If you visit Washington in the spring, try to include a stroll through the National Arboretum, the most comprehensive arboretum in the country. It boasts a collection of seventy species of dogwood. And do not forget the cherry trees!

Shortcomings: My reviewers all mentioned the meatless menu, which might be a problem for some attendees. Otherwise, no shortcomings were noted.

Getting In: The school's proximity to Washington, D.C., makes it a relatively popular destination.

Getting There: Either taxi or metro can be taken from Washington's National Airport to Takoma Park. One group of hostelers stayed overnight at a motel near Washington's international airport before proceeding to the college.

Washington can also be reached by Amtrak, interstate bus, or private car. The D.C. Union Railroad Station has recently been remodeled and might be worth a visit to see the refurbished marble floors and architecture reminiscent of Roman baths.

Massachusetts

Amherst—Hampshire College

Courses of Study: The Nuclear Age; Media Analysis; Linguistics

Quality of Instructors: Dynamic teachers whet students' intellectual curiosity.

Environment: Hampshire College is a relatively young school founded by a consortium of four neighboring institutions: Amherst, Smith, Mt. Holyoke, and the University of Massachusetts. It is an academically non-traditional school that encourages individualism.

Hampshire College has a wooded campus located in the Pioneer Valley near Amherst and Northampton. The school is ideally situated for enjoying the cultural attractions and special events at all four colleges, and a free shuttle bus provides transportation between the five schools. Unlike its more elite neighbors, the campus at Hampshire is not lush —in fact, it is rather plain.

Housing: The dormitories, built in apartment-style clusters, are shabby and unappealing and have the usual shared bath facilities.

Food: The cafeteria serves an excellent menu designed to please the health-conscious school population. "If you're not into sprouts you might find the meals on the light side."

Unique Attributes: The school boasts excellent recreational facilities. It even has an indoor, glass-enclosed swimming pool and a sauna. Hampshire is an unorthodox, small school that encourages creativity. "Hampshire," reported one pair of Elderhostelers, "usually does one serious subject in great depth, therefore it attracts an intellectually inquisitive, earnest group of Elderhostelers."

"One brilliant instructor pursues one subject to a fault. Even the participants are better educated than any other hostel we've attended," enthused another couple. The Pioneer Valley is a rich, scenic area along the Connecticut River with foliage that glows in both the spring and fall. Downtown Amherst is within walking distance of the campus, and Elderhostelers can enjoy the strip of ultra-chic shops, quaint cafés, and restaurants in town. They can also attend foreign films, concerts, and lectures at the other colleges in the area.

Shortcomings: The accommodations are not up to par.

Getting In: This is a very popular destination during the height of the fall foliage season. But early reservations are mandatory year-round.

Getting There: Buses and limousines carry passengers between the Springfield-Hartford Airport and Amherst, but this destination is easily reached by automobile over high-speed turnpikes.

Boston—Emmanuel College

Courses of Study: William Blake; The New Right; Prescription and Non-Prescription Drugs; Art as Autobiography; Politics and the Media; The Boston Woman—A Historical Overview

Quality of Instructors: A very scholarly teaching staff.

Environment: The college has a pleasant, tree-shaded campus right in the historic Back Bay area of the city. Boston is one of the country's most interesting cities; its narrow, winding streets are rich in history. Emmanuel was the first Catholic college for women in New England and is administered by an order of nuns who have relinquished wearing habits. My reviewers noted that religion was not intrusive in the program.

Housing: Comfortable double rooms with excellent shared-bath facilities.

Food: Very good college cafeteria.

Unique Attributes: Morning and evening classes are scheduled to leave the hostelers free time to enjoy the city's variety of experiences. Several museums and parks are within walking distance, and downtown Boston can be accessed by good local transportation. "The Cradle of Liberty" is rich in history. Paul Revere's House, Old North Church, and Faneuil Hall can be found on streets that retain the charm of colonial days. The remodeled Quincy Market and renovated waterfront wharves are wonderful examples of successful urban renewal projects.

Shortcomings: Can be very hot in summer. Bring a fan or check before registering to see if air-conditioning has been installed.

Getting In: Emmanuel's program has a good reputation, so there may be a large demand for space. My reviewers had no difficulty getting accepted.

Getting There: The school provides parking facilities for private cars should you choose to drive to Boston. The city is also served by Greyhound and Trailways bus, train, or plane to Logan International Airport.

Groton—Lawrence Academy

Courses of Study: Russian Culture; How Poetry Works; New England Landscape; American History

Quality of Instructors: A teaching staff of great communicators.

Environment: Groton is an affluent suburban community, and its broad, green lawns and picture-postcard landscape provide a backdrop for an elite boy's preparatory school. The lovely campus, just one hour's drive from Boston, has tennis courts, a swimming pool, and a very fine library.

Housing: Elderhostelers sleep in twin-bedded dormitory rooms with shared bathroom facilities.

Food: Meals are good and quantities ample.

Unique Attributes: Good field trips are arranged by staff. Hike in the woods one day and stroll through a bog on another. The Russian course instructor and his daughter host a Russian soirée for the reading of Maxim Gorky and Chekov by candlelight.

Shortcomings: The women's bathroom facilities are makeshift and therefore inadequate. My reviewers felt neglected by the lack of planned evening activities.

Getting In: My reviewers were accepted without any difficulties.

Getting There: The automobile drive from Boston is easy and pleasant. Logan Airport in Boston is a major international airport.

Northfield—Northfield Mt. Hermon School

Courses of Study: Shakespeare; Literature; Gardening; Geneology; American Film Comedies

Quality of Instructors: "Top drawer." "Superb." "Sometimes equaled but never surpassed." One five-year Northfield veteran wrote, "The skill and enthusiasm of the teachers is unrivaled in the Elderhostel movement."

Between-class socializing, Northfield-Mt. Hermon School, Northfield, Massachusetts.

East Hall, Northfield-Mt. Hermon School, Northfield, Massachusetts.

Environment: The green, rolling hills of this campus have a pleasing symmetry that typifies the best of New England. Two coeducational boarding schools make up one large community known as the Northfield Mt. Hermon School. The campus is a blend of old brick and more recent buildings that fit together like a lovely calendar picture whose backdrop is a charming view of the distant mountains. From the second and third floors of the dormitories, one can see the Connecticut River winding through the valley.

Housing: Third floor, non-air-conditioned rooms can be very uncomfortable during a heat spell, and some very old buildings are in dire need of interior paint, repair, and cleaning. However, one reviewer was intrigued by the wonderful old infirmary building in which she was housed. "It had ancient, 100-year-old, clawfooted bathtubs," she wrote.

Food: The Elderhostel program at Northfield Mt. Hermon is privileged to have its own kitchen, staff, and dining room. The menu is fancier and more plentiful than most Elderhostels. Fresh fruit, coffee, and cold drinks are available twenty-four hours a day.

Unique Attributes: The Elderhostel staff are superbly sensitive to the needs of an Elderhostel population. They are uniquely accessible and join the group at all meals and extracurricular activities. The atmosphere is one of mutual respect and appreciation among staff, teachers, and students.

The school's facilities are excellent. Dormitories and classroom buildings have congenial communal rooms and porches for lounging, an outdoor and an Olympic-size indoor swimming pool, and golf and tennis nearby.

For the most part, Northfield attracts serious-minded students of literature and Shakespeare. The area is physically picturesque, and evening activities are well planned. An extracurricular boat ride on the Connecticut River and picnic supper are enjoyable.

One admirer wrote, "This is a model to be emulated throughout the Elderhostel movement."

Shortcomings: Lack of air-conditioning or other cooling system in the dormitories, dining room, and theater can be brutal when New England suffers an unnaturally hot summer. Most of the Northfield residential buildings are very old and in need of refurbishing and a thorough cleaning. One ultra-fastidious reviewer, the mother of several Northfield alumni, was so offended by the grimy bathrooms and dust heaps in the bedrooms that she did not attend most classes.

Getting In: Northfield Mt. Hermon only holds its Elderhostel program for three weeks each summer, so early registration is a must. The program director boasts that Northfield has the highest reenrollment rate in Elderhostel.

Getting There: Northfield Mt. Hermon is best reached by automobile. Greenfield, Massachusetts—fifteen miles away—is served by Amtrak and Interstate bus lines. Eastern Airlines and Precision Air fly into Keene, New Hampshire's Dillant-Hopkins Airport, some twenty miles away.

Rowe—Rowe Conference Center

Courses of Study: Woodland Ecology; Perennial Flower Gardens; Broadway Musicals

Quality of Instructors: This unusual group of horticulturalists and naturalists was rated excellent.

Environment: The center is tucked away in the mountains within walking distance of a small New England village on the Mohawk Trail, a scenic highway that runs from central Massachusetts to the New York border. An old Indian path that follows the Cold River, the Mohawk Trail has switchbacks along sheer ravines and passes through a few tiny villages. The Conference Center is part of a one-thousand-acre wildlife preserve.

Rowe has a peaceful village green bordered with steepled churches and an old town hall. Low stone walls mark the property lines and edge the roads. The countryside is particularly spectacular after the first frost turns the white birch leaves to gold and clothes the maple trees in scarlet.

Housing: The old New England farmhouse in which Elderhostelers are housed has adequate, shared rooms and one large bath. Privacy is minimal.

Food: "Absolutely beyond belief!" Homemade breads, cookies, desserts, and artistic salads are served family style.

Unique Attributes: Either try to arrange a fall foliage trip to join the leaf-lovers or go in April, when the sap begins to run in the sugar maple trees. Make it soon before this wonderful annual harvest has been completely mechanized, the sap gathered through ugly plastic tubing instead of charming old wooden buckets.

Participants set tables, bus, wash dishes, and scrub large pots and pans. This activity, though resented by some hostelers, in a large measure promotes a real sense of family among participants. Wonderful opportunities are offered for hiking, canoeing, and photographing the countryside. The sweet fragrance of the woodlands will remain in your memory long after you have returned home.

Shortcomings: Physically, this is a very strenuous program. The distances walked are very long. It is essential that the attendees be very congenial because of the elbow-to-elbow KP duty.

Getting In: During the height of the fall foliage season, this program develops long waiting lists. Early registration is recommended.

Getting There: Rowe can be reached conveniently only by automobile. One can fly to Hartford/Springfield to the south, take an Amtrak train to Greenfield, or fly to Albany, New York, and rent a car at any of those destinations.

Michigan

Ann Arbor—University of Michigan

Courses of Study: Interpersonal Communication; Emily Dickinson; Satellite Photo-Mapping; Comfort in the Concert Hall; Blues, Jazz and Ragtime; A Cultural Perspective; A Recorded History of American Country-Western Hillbilly Music

Quality of Instructors: "Fabulous," enthused one couple, who said they were "unequivocally sold on the intellectual stimulation of Elderhosteling in a huge, world-class institution."

Environment: Ann Arbor is a small city that revolves around the university and its 34,000 students. It is an ideal college community; canopies of oaks and maples cloak the sidewalks and turn-of-the-century homes edge the streets of the city. Michigan, before the loggers came, was a densely forested state. It still has woodlands, but they are now efficiently managed. Ann Arbor is located in the industrialized area of the state near Detroit, the automobile-manufacturing capital of the United States.

Housing: Elderhostelers reside in non-air-conditioned dormitories with communal bath facilities.

Food: The college cafeteria offers a wide selection.

Unique Attributes: "The most intellectually stimulating Elderhostel of the eight we attended," was the effusive evaluation of a pair of devoted hostelers. "We enjoyed a lively exchange of ideas." The state of Michigan has a long tradition of respect for education so it is not suprising to find the state university with an outstanding reputation. The school's athletic facilities include a golf course and several swimming pools. The upper peninsula of Michigan has long, harsh winters but the lower peninsula, the Ann Arbor and Detroit areas, are protected from the arctic Canadian chills by the waters of the Great Lakes.

Shortcomings: "No way," according to our reviewers.

Getting In: This program is usually oversubscribed, but it is well worth suffering through the uncertainty of waiting lists or chancing the lottery at the national headquarters registration department.

Getting There: Detroit is a major transportation center with frequent service of jet planes, interstate buses, and trains.

Rochester Hills—Michigan Christian College

Courses of Study: You Can Make The Difference!; The Most Remarkable Book in Existence; But I Thought a Canon Was a Big Gun!

Quality of Instructors: "Jovial and very articulate." "Top-notch academics."

Environment: The college has a delightfully small, friendly campus that surrounds two lakes and the Clinton River. It is a coeducational Christian school that prohibits smoking anywhere on its grounds. Rochester Hills lies just a half hour's drive north of Detroit where the winds from Lake Michigan make the area one of the cloudiest sections of the United States. Michigan is a state with two peninsulas separated by Lake Michigan. It is a vacationland of 11,000 lakes and rivers, and the upper peninsula is best known as "the shores of Gitchee Gumee."

Housing: Alma Gatewood Dormitory is designed with one bathroom for each pair of double rooms.

Food: The college cafeteria is very well managed, and a choice of two entrées is offered to diners. The cafeteria is catered by Marriott.

Unique Attributes: The college president establishes this program's uniquely convivial atmosphere when he rolls out the welcome mat at the opening orientation meeting. This Michigan-style Willkommen creates a special esprit among Elderhostelers. After the congenial kickoff, students mingle freely with the faculty and are in a receptive frame of mind for all the courses. The music instructor enhances his lectures with wonderful recordings; the course on interpersonal relations is a lively exchange of ideas; and the evening on-campus programs are great.

Shortcomings: Smokers would definitely have a problem on this campus.

Getting In: My reviewers attended this particular program as a second or third choice when they were unable to get in to Ann Arbor. Michigan Christian College proved to be an unexpected treat, "a wonderful suprise—we'd recommend it unconditionally."

Getting There: Take public transportation to Detroit and rent a car for the twenty-four-mile drive to Rochester Hills if you wish to explore some of upper Michigan's lakes and rivers.

Minnesota

Duluth—College of St. Scholastica

Courses of Study: Bible; Musical Theater (Broadway plays, musical comedies)

Quality of Instructors: Excellent. "When the nun scheduled to teach us was hospitalized, we were moved to the University of Minnesota-Duluth campus for the musicals course without missing a beat." "The music instructor was fantastic—he lectured right from the piano bench."

Environment: Duluth, a city of 82,700 people, is just a bus ride away from the school. The city buses conveniently stop right on the campus. Duluth, an interesting city, was named for a French fur trader and was settled by Scandinavian and German immigrants. Duluth is on the far western edge of Lake Superior, and it is awesome to watch oceangoing vessels sail out of the city headed for the Atlantic Ocean—some twenty-four hundred water miles away. The college sits at the top of a hill with a wonderful view of the lake.

Housing: Elderhostelers stay in modern college dormitories with showers and baths down the hall.

Food: Plenty of good but not fancy meals are served.

Unique Attributes: Very fine evening programs are offered at St. Scholastica, while academic programs are handled cooperatively with the University of Minnesota in Duluth. The Bible study course can be particularly stimulating when active participants are from different traditions and bring diverse points of view to the discussion.

Shortcomings: An automobile is needed if one wishes to see the off-campus sights of North Shore, Gooseberry Falls, and Split Rock State Forest. Some beds have "weak" mattresses, but one reviewer suggested that attendees request bed boards or an extra firm mattress in advance. If the management can fill all such requests the problem is not irreparable.

Getting In: Even though this college can accommodate a fair-sized group, early registrations are necessary. This one gets rave reviews.

Getting There: Duluth can be reached by all forms of public transportation. Northwest Airlines has frequent flight schedules.

Lake Burnside—Vermilion Community College

Courses of Study: Fur Trading; Flora and Fauna; Exploring the North Woods; History of the North Woods

Paddling a canoe similar to those of 1800s fur traders, Burnside Lake, Minnesota. (Photo by Bill Behrends)

Quality of Instructors: A very pleasant couple conducts the program. They enhance the courses with craft and candle-making demonstrations.

Environment: This program is given at Camp Northland, a YMCA camp on the wooded shore of Lake Burnside, eighteen miles north of Ely. This is remote woodlands, almost on the Minnesota/Canadian border.

Housing: Elderhostelers are housed in double- and triple-occupancy heated cabins. Toilet and shower facilities are in a centralized building. Classes and activities are conducted in a communal lodge.

Food: Plain, home-cooked food is served in a lakeside dining hall.

Unique Attributes: Because of the nature of the institution, this program has daily flag raising and lowering ceremonies as well as a prayer before each meal, including the evening campfires. This program offers a wonderful week of spiritual rebirth and renewal as well as an opportunity to enjoy sunsets, stars, and sunrises in a lovely setting. When not in class studying wildlife preservation and protection of our natural lands, Elderhostelers are free to paddle the canoes, swim in the lake, fish in the ponds, and sail.

Shortcomings: The centralized shower and toilet facilities are some distance from the sleeping cabins— a problem for night usage.

Getting In: No problems reported.

Getting There: Private vehicles are necessary for traveling to Lake Burnside. One could fly to Duluth and rent a car or board a motor coach there.

St. Joseph—College of St. Benedict

Courses of Study: The Old Testament; Making Memories; Fiction

Quality of Instructors: "An excellent group of pedagogues who piqued our interest."

Environment: St. Joseph is a very small town with a population of barely 3,000 people. St. Cloud, five miles away, has a shopping center and good restaurants. This is the area of Minnesota memorialized by Garrison Keillor, the radio humorist, in his "Lake Wobegon Days" program. St. Joseph may be "the town that time forgot, that the decades cannot improve." The area was founded by Norwegians and Germans, and the crops grown are wheat, corn, oats, and alfalfa. St. Benedict is a four-year Benedictine college located seventy miles northwest of the Twin Cities.

Housing: The accommodations are all modern, well kept, clean, and comfortable. Some of the dormitories and apartments are new and in excellent condition.

Food: Well-prepared meals are served in a ground-level, air-conditioned dining room that is conveniently located adjacent to the dormitories and classrooms.

Unique Attributes: The small-town environment is charming, but St. Joseph is just an hour and a half drive to the Twin Cities. The trip can also be made by public bus, although only one trip daily is scheduled each way. St. Benedict is a liberal arts school for women. St. John's University in Collegeville is the brother school for men, and St. Cloud State University is just five miles away. Minnesota is a pleasant suprise for people from the south, west and east, and don't forget—Minnesota has 10,000 lakes!

Shortcomings: No shortcomings reported.

Getting In: There is a waiting list every summer for this much-in-demand program. One pair of Elder-hostelers wrote that they tried three times before they were accepted.

Getting There: St. Joseph can be reached by interstate bus or commuter flights on Midwest Aviation.

Winona—St. Mary's College

Courses of Study: The River (Mississippi); Jazz of the 20s and 30s; Physical Fitness

Quality of Instructors: The quality varies from well prepared and well informed to a "warm, interesting maverick whose digressions were as fascinating as his subject matter."

"Our physical fitness instructor dared us to be young again!"

Environment: St. Mary's has a beautiful 350-acre campus. Downtown Winona is only two miles away, yet the campus is secluded in the Hiawatha Valley. Do you remember how Hiawatha in Longfellow's poem "crossed the mighty Mississippi" and stood on the meadow at "the Great Red Pipestone Quarry"? You can see both the quarry and the Mississippi on this adventure.

Housing: Elderhostelers are housed in very adequate, traditional dormitories. They are not fancy, nor are they air-conditioned.

Food: A vast variety of excellent food is served in an air-conditioned dining room. The final banquet is an elegant affair with linen cloths and napkins and silver-plated samovars.

Unique Attributes: St. Mary's is a small college under the auspices of the Brothers of the Christian Schools and has a Catholic view. It is located only 120 miles from the Twin Cities of St. Paul and Minneapolis. The romance is not all gone from the upper Mississippi River. It is still home to modern barges hauling cargoes and is the largest resting spot in North America for bald eagles, whistling swans and falcons. Watch out! Winter comes early, can be bitter cold, and stays late in Minnesota.

"Terrific staff. Did a great job of fine tuning our muscles and tendons!"

Shortcomings: The shower room can be too messy for fastidious Elderhostelers, but the problem could be solved with the use of less skimpy shower curtains. The lack of air-conditioning in the dormitories makes them uncomfortable during a summer heat wave.

Getting In: No problems reported.

Getting There: Good public transportation is available, and Winona is situated on major thruways. Rochester, Minnesota, has the nearest airport.

Missouri

Hannibal—Hannibal-La Grange College

Courses of Study: Mark Twain Studies

Quality of Instructors: A group of teachers who bring a fresh perspective and enthusiasm to a familiar subject.

Environment: Hannibal-La Grange is a Southern Baptist institution. Smoking on campus and the use of alcoholic beverages are prohibited. The town has been immortalized as the birthplace of Mark Twain. It sits on the shores of "Old Muddy," the brown Mississippi River.

Housing: Elderhostelers are housed in very comfortable air-conditioned buildings.

Food: The school practices Mark Twain's dictum, "Nothing helps scenery like ham and eggs."

Unique Attributes: Hannibal is a living memorial to the town's most famous son, Samuel Langhorne Clemens. It has a Mark Twain Museum, the Mark Twain Cave, Jackson's Island, and even a Mark Twain Lake with a picnic grove on its shore. The famous fence is marked with a plaque and stands next to Clemens's boyhood home. A towering bronze statue of Twain looks over his beloved Mississippi from a park, and a statue of Tom Sawyer and Huck Finn honors the adventurous boys. One can almost feel the presence of Huck Finn and Injun Joe. The course covers Twain's historical fiction, social fiction, essays, humor, travel books, and short "tall" stories, as well as the better-known classics. The school has a nine-hole golf course and lovely wooded walking paths from which one can watch the streamlined river boats that have replaced the stern- and side-wheelers traveling the Mississippi.

Getting In: None of my reviewers reported any problems.

Getting There: One has the option of using all forms of public transportation to get to Hannibal. Fly to St. Louis for connections to Quincy, Illinois, on a commuter airline; Quincy is twenty miles from Hannibal, so one can finish this journey by bus, limo, or rented automobile.

Potosi—YMCA of the Ozarks

Courses of Study: Literature and Folklore of the Ozarks; Waterways of the Ozarks; Natural History of the Ozarks

Quality of Instructors: The courses are taught by naturalists and folklorists sensitive to the importance of our history and variety of the landscape.

Environment: The camp is situated in 3,000 acres of oak and pine forest in the low Ozark Mountains, only eighteen hundred feet above sea level. This is romantic country where the buffalo roamed. Potosi is south of St. Louis, a city frequently considered the boundary between the East and the West.

Housing: Elderhostelers stay at Trout Lodge in top-notch accommodations with private baths and queen-size beds. The lodge also has a lovely view of Sunnen Lake. The classrooms, dining room, and sleeping quarters are all in the same building.

Food: My reviewers gave the meals high praise.

Unique Attributes: Wonderful field trips and guided nature hikes are taken to see rocky bluffs, caves, and clear, cold springs. The autumn foliage glows on the hickory, oak, and maple trees on the bluffs. Elderhostelers may hike the trails blazed by Daniel Boone. The course in Ozark history and literature helps us understand from whence we have come and thereby gives us a better sense of where we are going.

Shortcomings: Summers in the Ozarks can be hot, humid, and uncomfortable.

Getting In: No problems were reported with over-booking.

Getting There: St. Louis is a major transportation center with excellent air service, a railroad station, and bus terminal. Transportation from St. Louis can be arranged to Potosi.

Nebraska

Cherry County National Forest near Halsey, Nebraska—Kearney State

Courses of Study: Listen to the Land (a history of hardy pioneers pressing West to establish homes); Ecology of the Sandhills; Cultural and Social Life of Homesteaders

Quality of Instructors: Excellent to superior. One much-traveled couple wrote, "Of all the Elderhostels we have attended, these Kearney State instructors are the most knowledgeable."

Environment: The 4H camp is nestled within the rolling hills of the only man-made national park in the United States. The park is one of Teddy Roosevelt's conservation plans, and all the trees were planted and the seeding done during his administration. Nebraska is not a state frequented by tourists, and even many ardent travelers do not know this land. One must get off the interstate to discover the real America, to see the regional architecture of a farm combine, barn, or grain elevator. Sightseeing in Nebraska means hay, cattle, and sand dunes. This is America's heartland, where the spirit of the pioneers and frontiersmen still lingers.

Housing: The Elderhostelers are housed in a 4H camp with double cabins and each pair of rooms sharing a bath. Extra washbowls are built into each bedroom. The accommodations are rustic but adequate.

Food: Good wholesome food is served in a nice dining hall.

Unique Attributes: This Elderhostel is addressed to nature lovers and photographers. My reviewers report the presentations as outstanding, so mesmerizing they felt themselves a part of the westward movement and settlement! The physical plant of this particular camp is more comfortable than most woodland retreats. There are paved walkways to all cabins, and the Elderhostelers' luggage and belongings are transported from parking lot to cabins by motorized carts operated by 4Hers.

Shortcomings: My reviewers had a few minor suggestions, such as better lighting on the cabin paths and a more convenient parking lot.

Getting In: This program has a maximum capacity of twenty-two attendees, so early registration is absolutely necessary.

Getting There: This is a remote area in the middle of the state best reached by automobile. The closest airport is in North Platte, Nebraska—not very close. This airport handles commuter flights from Omaha.

New Jersey

Wayne—William Paterson College

Courses of Study: Evolution; TV Workshop; Carmen the Opera through the Years; Folk Music

Quality of Instructors: An impressive group of media professionals augment the teaching staff.

Environment: William Paterson College has 250 wooded acres of campus for its ninety-five hundred students but is essentially an urban campus. It boasts superb facilities: a science complex, a performing and visual arts center, a health spa, and its own radio/color TV studios. Wayne, a city of 50,000, is located in the heart of New Jersey's industrialized, heavily populated metropolitan zone. It is a city noted for its textile manufacturing and dyeing industries.

Housing: Elderhostelers are housed in dormitory rooms that are dingy and dirty but air-conditioned.

Food: "Awful." One couple complained that they were mixed with a group of youngsters using the campus as a basketball camp. The menu was geared to the taste of the basketballers, and the campus dining room was painfully noisy with very loud rock music pouring out of the loudspeakers.

Unique Attributes: Paterson is a school that educates the inner-city youngsters from Paterson and many nearby communities. Elderhostelers are exposed to the career-oriented educational goals of the school and its unique achievements. The hands-on Elderhostel TV workshop actually produces talk shows for WPC-TV, while the same experience prepares undergraduates for jobs in the media. The Elderhostel field trips, to view urban-renewal minority housing projects in town as well as the Paterson waterfalls, are unusual experiences. The waterfall is historically significant— it is the reason Paterson was chosen by Alexander Hamilton to be the first industrial city of the fledgling United States. Calling New Jersey "The Garden State" is a cruel hoax. However, when one drives west on Route 80, past the factories and odiferous oil refineries, the ribbons of concrete give way to greenery, lakes, and elegant suburban towns.

Shortcomings: The food needs much improvement. One reviewer complained, "Our group of forty-five was given Fruit Loops for breakfast and Heros for lunch."

Getting In: No problems reported.

Getting There: Wayne lies just across the Hudson River from New York City. It is served by commuter buses with frequent schedules to the New York City bus terminal. In addition, it can be reached by major or commuter railroad lines, airplane to Newark International Airport, and multilane arterial highways.

New Mexico

Albuquerque/Rio Rancho—New Mexico Community Foundation/ Rio Rancho Inn

Courses of Study: History of Pueblo Indians; Old Albuquerque; Natural History of New Mexico; New Mexican Authors

Quality of Instructors: An excellent group of instructors from the University of New Mexico and the College of Santa Fe teach the courses at the Inn.

Environment: The Inn is situated in the country, ten miles from downtown Albuquerque, a city of 450,000. Albuquerque is the state's largest city, renowned for its Old Town. Nearby barrio residents still farm one-acre plots of land. This historic Old Town surrounds a plaza where some of New Mexico's best artists and artisans exhibit their work in shops and galleries, and Indians from nearby pueblos spread their wares on blankets. Unfortunately, the rest of Albuquerque is filled with commercial highway strips of gas stations, fast-food emporiums, and motels, but it does lie on a bend of the Rio Grande. The climate is high, dry, and invigorating.

Housing: Elderhostelers enjoy private motel rooms with private baths! The very pleasant first-floor accommodations are air-conditioned, too.

Food: "Kitchen management at the Inn was unfamiliar with the dietary needs of seniors and served meals high in salt and cholesterol. After we complained, the food changed for the better. Ours was the first Elderhostel at this destination. Hopefully it will improve."

Unique Attributes: "We learned how to spell Albuquerque!"

In and around the city one can see classic gems of pueblo architecture with its horizontal lines, thick adobe walls, rounded corners and earth tones.

In Old Town one can visit San Miguel, reputed to be the oldest church in the United States, and the Museum of New Mexico with exhibits on Indian life and culture.

Shortcomings: Staff at the Inn are inexperienced at Elderhosteling but seem to be willing to learn. Problems were noted with the food, insufficient field trips, and no evening activities. Since the Inn is ten miles from town, Elderhostelers without automobiles "felt like second-class citizens."

Getting In: Moderately difficult now but should become very popular because of the private bath facilities.

Getting There: Albuquerque has good transcontinental air service as well as interstate bus service and trains. The Rio Rancho administrators meet Elderhostelers at the airport.

Santa Fe—College of Santa Fe (formerly The Christian Brothers College)

Courses of Study: Opera; Science Fiction as Literature; History of New Mexico; Southwest Indians; Santa Fe Trail and Expansion

Quality of Instructors: Very good. The classes are intellectually stimulating and thought-provoking.

Environment: The college is located right in town within walking distance of shopping and restaurants. The town of Santa Fe offers a wealth of musical treats. The campus, however, is shamefully neglected, and "the library, beautiful to look at, is as unfriendly as the rest of the place."

Housing: Elderhostelers stay in college dormitories with semiprivate baths. The accommodations are perfectly adequate, though small.

Food: Chow hounds, steer clear of this one! Service is terrible, and the food is offered in a most unattractive, barnlike army Quonset hut. "Give them a D," wrote one attendee. Fortunately, an assortment of fast-food emporiums is located just a stone's throw from the college. I observed a few portly gentlemen making daily excursions to the Big Boy on the corner, while other hostelers had pizza delivered to the dorm.

Unique Attributes: Santa Fe is an artist's mecca with a labyrinth of shops and art galleries. In Santa Fe one can discover the beauty of New Mexican architecture, a blend of Indian, Spanish, and Anglo. The Museum of

Festival at Indian Pueblo, Santa Fe, New Mexico.

Folk Art is a must! Arrangements are made for a night at the world-renowned opera in the summer, but you must buy your own tickets. Some good sight-seeing tours are included in the registration package. Some groups attended theater, and others made field trips to visit petroglyphs that were well worth the extra cost.

The backstage tour of the Sante Fe Opera is a special bird's-eye view of the mechanics of building sets and creating costumes—a not-to-be-missed thrill for opera buffs. The advance mailing of tourist attractions is very informative.

Shortcomings: If you need hand-holding, it is not available at Santa Fe. The program director is invisible. No attempt is made by the college to foster any group camaraderie among the Elderhostelers. The program is mismanaged.

The unclean campus and unfriendly staff (other than Elderhostel teachers) are abysmal. To thoroughly enjoy the sights and sounds of Santa Fe, a car is necessary.

Getting In: This is a very popular destination, but they offer Elderhostel programs forty-eight weeks a year, so waiting lists should not be too long. In addition, they host very large (too large, according to some panelists) groups at one time. From coast to coast, Santa Fe is rated high on the list of desirable places to go.

Getting There: The nearest airport is Albuquerque, but public transportation is available from the airport to Santa Fe. An automobile is recommended if one wishes to enjoy all of Santa Fe's special attractions.

A pair of Elderhostelers from the East Coast recommend flying and renting a car in Albuquerque.

Las Cruces—New Mexico State University

Courses of Study: Beginning Conversational Spanish; A Close-Up of China Today; Understanding Practical Concepts in Mathematics

Quality of Instructors: Adequate but not inspiring.

Environment: Las Cruces is the second-largest city in New Mexico, located some forty-five miles north of El

Paso. It exhibits a pleasant blend of the three dominant cultures: Indian, Spanish, and Anglo. The Organ Mountains lie to the east and the Rio Grande to the west. The Elderhostel program takes place in a rural setting outside of the city at the Holy Cross Retreat, a beautiful old Spanish hacienda on the Rio Grande. New Mexico State University has a 6,000-acre campus reputed to be one of the largest in the world.

Housing: Elderhostelers are accommodated in double rooms with private baths.

Food: An agreeable array of college fare is presented.

Unique Attributes: NMSU is a state school with an undergraduate body of 11,000 students. It boasts an eighteen-hole golf course, lighted tennis courts, and two swimming pools—one indoor and one outdoor.

Shortcomings: This location is brutally hot in the summer. The school buildings are equipped with evaporative coolers, but they are apparently not adequate for the intensity of the summer temperatures.

"Don't bother going to this one!" grumbled an unhappy couple.

Getting In: If this program was ever oversubscribed in the past, it won't be in the future.

Getting There: Greyhound and Continental Trailways buses have service to Las Cruces, or one can fly to El Paso International Airport. Of course, a car is the easiest method of getting there.

Taos—Las Palomas de Taos (a nonprofit organization)

Courses of Study: Mabel Luhan's Art Colony; Archaeology of New Mexico

Quality of Instructors: No consensus among reviewers. Opinions ranged from "well educated in the subject matter" to "enthusiastic" to "disappointing."

Environment: Taos lies in a valley whose natural beauty, magical sunlight, and red-colored canyons are like an artist's palette. The town is small, quiet, and quaint. Taos is not just a collection of sights to be seen—it is an experience to be shared and felt.

Mabel Dodge Luhan was the mistress of a Taos grand salon in the twenties and thirties. She gathered writers such as Willa Cather and artists such as Georgia O'Keefe and John Marin to establish a uniquely American art form that received its inspiration from from our own natives, the American Indian. Mabel Dodge Luhan created an oasis of culture in the Southwest.

Housing: A small group of Elderhostelers can be accommodated in Mabel Dodge Luhan's hacienda or in the pueblo. The mansion has one "gorgeous room that sleeps five and several other elegant, twin-bedded rooms." The hacienda has been designated a "historical place in the arts."

Elderhostelers put up in motels have been so disgruntled that they bowed out of the program immediately. If one is housed in the motel, a car is a necessity. Check

on your housing accommodations when you register—
it is luck of the draw whether you will win "gorgeous"
or "impossible."

Food: Very good regional food is beautifully served in
the mansion dining room. An American Indian cook
prepares Southwestern specialties and teaches her
culinary skills to interested Elderhostelers.

Unique Attributes: Taos is a paradise for art lovers,
particularly for lovers of southwestern art. Local
artists are invited regularly as guests of the program.

The homelike atmosphere and small number in the
group establish a delightful spirit of congeniality. "At
the end of five days we felt like old friends in a familiar
place." The group interacts from an early-morning
exercise class through to the evening's simple activities. A fine reading list is mailed to participants prior
to the event and helps them become immersed in a
beautiful, different culture.

The Elderhostel hosts are very accommodating. They
escort the group to festivals and dances at the Taos
Indian Pueblo and to area museums.

Shortcomings: Overbooking creates many housing
problems. Elderhostelers report being accommodated
in inadequate, inhospitable guest houses as well as the
motels noted above. "If you're tall, watch out for low
ceilings!"

The weather in summer is hot but dry, and the high
altitude can be difficult for some Elderhostelers.

Getting In: This is a very popular program and has
limited space. It is absolutely necessary to enroll early.
One woman wrote that of ten Elderhostels, Taos is her

favorite. She returned a second time to determine if Taos is more beautiful in the winter or summer. "It's a draw," she wrote.

Getting There: Taos is accessible by major airline to Albuquerque or bus to Taos. The commuter airline Mesa Air also makes the run between Albuquerque and Taos.

Silver City—Bear Mountain Guest Ranch

Courses of Study: Bird-Watching for Beginners; Geology; From Pithouse to Suburb—Historical South-western Experience

Quality of Instructors: The quality varied from imperfect to excellent, with the professor from the local college given a rating of excellent, a forest ranger applauded for his skill, down to the owner of the ranch, whose teaching ability was sharply criticized. A more charitable couple found the proprietress a uniquely colorful character whose bird-watching expeditions were entertaining, if not informative.

Environment: Silver City is a sparsely settled area of a sparsely settled state. The ranch itself is spread over a very pretty area with modern, hacienda-style buildings dotting the hills. The ranch is situated at 6,250 feet above sea level.

Housing: The Elderhostelers are housed in various types of accommodations: a lodge, adequate private cabins, and some less comfortable abodes.

Food: The proprietress cooked the meals for the Elderhostel program. "Home-cooked but inadequate," complained one couple of panelists.

Unique Attributes: The location of Silver City seems to be this program's greatest asset. The city is located just minutes away from the Gila Cliff Dwellings National Monument, where five natural caves are situated high on the face of a cliff. The dwellings were built by the Mogollon Indians between 1170 and 1350. One of the caves can actually be visited over a steep trail and steps. The Silver City Museum is a Victorian house with a square tower that once was the home of a prospector who struck it rich in the 1870s. Mannequins in period attire evoke the mining boom. The location also offers access to present-day copper mines.

The ranch can only accommodate twenty-four Elderhostelers, which encourages a congenial atmosphere. The program started each day with a before-breakfast exercise class, followed by an afternoon field trip, and some local entertainment is arranged for every evening.

Shortcomings: This program is run by a for-profit ranch rather than a university. The focus unfortunately seems to be on profit rather than on learning.

Getting In: My reviewers had no difficulty making reservations.

Getting There: Silver City is definitely off the beaten path, but it can be reached by bus from Las Cruces. Greyhound and Trailways bus lines serve Las Cruces, or one can fly to El Paso, Texas.

New York

Alfred—Alfred University

Courses of Study: Sculpture; Mathematics; American Music

Quality of Instructors: Scholars rated "wonderful to outstanding!"

Environment: Alfred is a small village in the Finger Lakes Region of New York State. The area is characterized by gracious living, vineyards, and freshwater pastimes. The environment is rural and pastoral with innumerable lakes and streams and apple orchards. Queen Anne's lace blooms along the roadsides, farmers sell apples off the tailgates of their trucks, and the trees have a last flashy fling each fall before the bleakness of winter arrives.

Alfred was the first coed university in the state of New York. The town is a small, self-contained college town that is home to just twenty-four hundred students.

Housing: Elderhostelers stay in traditional dormitories that are more than adequate.

Food: Meals are served cafeteria style in the school dining room. They are well presented and there are many choices at every meal.

Unique Attributes: The Finger Lakes were created a million years ago when ice masses formed long narrow lakes with deep gorges. The area is topographically unique and boasts about its 1,000 waterfalls.

Very good evening entertainment is scheduled for the Elderhostelers. Programs include chamber music concerts, carillon concerts, and village band performances in town. The forty-seven-bell carillon used for demonstrations and concerts is the pride and joy of Alfred College. The Davis Memorial Carillon contains the oldest carillon bells in the Western Hemisphere. Although a small school, Alfred has excellent facilities: a computer center, an observatory with five telescopes, and seven tennis courts. The student body produces fine theatrical and dance programs, and popular entertainers and rock stars visit the campus, too. The Elderhostel staff, director, and assistants received rave reviews. "Considerate, helpful, courteous and caring" was one of the compliments I heard. "A delightful experience—A in every area," a much-traveled Elderhosteler wrote. She listed this as her favorite destination after attending Elderhostels all over the United States and abroad.

Shortcomings: No weaknesses reported, although I would caution attendees to be prepared with "bug dope" for the six-week black fly infestation in early spring.

Getting In: No difficulties reported, but after these hosannas, I would advise early registration.

Getting There: Most area visitors tour by automobile, using the New York Thruway. Greyhound Bus has service to the Finger Lakes area, and there is a small airport at Elmira/Corning.

Bronxville—Concordia College

Courses of Study: Dead Sea Scrolls; Philosophy; Jazz

Quality of Instructors: "Top drawer." "Skilled interpreters of difficult material."

Environment: Concordia is a small Lutheran school with an enrollment of just 385 men and women. The thirty-acre campus of quiet, tree-shaded paths and gentle rolling hills lies a mere fifteen miles north of New York City. This attractive campus sits right in the heart of Bronxville/Scarsdale, a jewel of New York suburbia, polished and precious and full of imposing old mansions. The Bronxville/Scarsdale area is for the affluent and privileged.

Housing: The dormitories are clean and comfortable.

Food: "Abundant," according to one reviewer. Even though this is a church-affiliated college, wine is served at the Elderhostel welcome and farewell dinners.

Unique Attributes: Bronxville is just twenty-eight minutes by commuter train from Grand Central Station in New York City. Concordia is an ideal location for joining the hustle-bustle of the "city that never sleeps." The Elderhostel director is most hospitable, charming, and entertaining. He runs an excellent program.

Shortcomings: No problems reported.

Getting In: Despite Bronxville's location in Westchester County just outside of New York City, the Concordia program has not been reported as oversubscribed.

Getting There: Westchester County has its own airport used by feeder lines if one wishes to make connections from La Guardia or Kennedy in New York City. Commuter train is also available, as noted above.

Lake Keuka—Keuka College

Courses of Study: Poetry Writing and Reading; Physical Fitness; German Anti-Nazi Underground

Quality of Instructors: Good to excellent—a stimulating faculty.

Environment: Keuka College has a small, picturesque, 173-acre campus right on the western shore of Lake Keuka. The school has an enrollment of only 500 women. This lovely freshwater lake is used extensively for fishing and canoeing. Views from the college campus include sailboats, sunsets, and fishing skiffs. The campus is a fine place for frazzled city dwellers to find some tranquility.

Housing: Elderhostelers sleep in typical dormitory rooms with one communal bathroom on each floor. "But these are cleaner than most," wrote one couple after their second visit to Keuka College. The bedrooms are all second- and third-floor rooms without benefit of elevator.

Food: The cafeteria provides more than adequate, good food.

Unique Attributes: Elderhostelers can swim in Lake Keuka, a clear, clean, blue lake just a short walk from the dormitory. South of Lake Keuka lies the town of Elmira, where Mark Twain spent twenty summers and wrote *The Adventures of Huckleberry Finn*. Twain referred to Elmira as "the Garden of Eden." The area is renowned for its vineyards and large wineries. In 1829 the Reverend William Bostwick planted a few grapevines near the shore of Lake Keuka. The grapes flourished in the local topsoil and ideal weather conditions. In the late 1880s, a large wine company was built in the area.

Shortcomings: Several attendees had difficulty doing the physical-fitness routines in the non-air-conditioned gymnasium.

Getting In: The programs do not seem to be oversubscribed.

Getting There: Most people enjoy touring the lakes region by automobile, although Greyhound Bus is available. If one wishes to fly, the nearest airport is in Elmira/Corning, and Saranac Lake has an airport served by Piedmont Airlines.

Oswego—State University of New York at Oswego

Courses of Study: Is Anyone Out There? (life elsewhere in the universe); Nutrition,Vitamins, and Drugs; American Musical Theater; Shakespeare's Women; The Great Lakes; Today's Grand Piano

Quality of Instructors: A broad array of mind-enlarging courses taught by excellent professors.

Environment: The campus of SUNY at Oswego is a modern, tree-lined complex that stretches along the southern shore of Lake Ontario. It is a 700-acre residential campus, and the school's enrollment is about 6,000 students.

The area has been immortalized by the adventures of the frontiersman, Leather-Stocking, in James Fenimore Cooper's *Pathfinder*. Oswego is a beautiful, medium-sized city of 20,000 people on Lake Ontario, forty miles northwest of Syracuse. Oswego has been declared a National Historic District, and it is surrounded by green, round-topped hills. In season, the restocked lake is thick with trawlers fishing for Chinook and coho salmon.

Housing: Elderhostelers are housed in very comfortable dormitories.

Food: The food is good, plentiful, and nicely presented, and the end-of-the-school week is celebrated with a lavish banquet.

Unique Attributes: One couple, veteran travelers to Oswego, voted this their number-one favorite destination. "Would recommend it highly."

The State University seems to have superb facilities for both recreation and education. The music program is enhanced with live performances, there is a dinner theater on the premises, and all the side trips are interesting and well organized. An Oswego "must see" is the Tioga Gardens, a solar-domed conservatory that houses a fabulous herb garden and lily ponds.

Shortcomings: None reported.

Getting In: No difficulties now, but perhaps after this rave review the program may become more popular, and early registration will be required.

Getting There: Oswego is best reached by automobile over interstate highways, but it also can be approached by feeder airlines, bus, or train.

Paul Smith—Paul Smith's College

Courses of Study: Casino Gambling; Wilderness in American Literature; The Adirondacks

Quality of Instructors: "Pretty bad. Give them a D-plus."

Environment: The fifty-acre campus sits on the shore of lovely St. Regis Lake, surrounded by wilderness mountain streams and trails. The lake is in the Adirondacks, not far from Lake Placid. This area of the Adirondacks is known for wild scenery and tumbling streams. Paul Smith is a small coed school whose students major in forestry and hotel or restaurant management.

Housing: The accommodations are very pleasant. Elderhostelers stay in private rooms with private baths.

Food: Sometimes Elderhostelers must share a cafeteria with forestry students who like to have rock music blaring over loudspeakers at mealtimes. One unhappy couple reported that they were moved—not too cordially—to an adjacent dining room after repeated requests to have the volume lowered. This intrusive discomfort might be considered just a petty annoyance to some individuals. I did not receive any complaints about the quantity or quality of food, however. In fact, since restaurant management is one of the curriculum majors, one might expect gourmet-style comestibles.

Unique Attributes: The Adirondack Mountains are by a statute of 1894 a "forever wild" wilderness, yet they are an easy drive from the major cities of the northeast. The mountains are most beautiful in the spring when the trees are budding or in the fall when the hills are washed with orange and amber hues. St. Regis Lake offers excellent facilities for swimming, canoeing, and fishing, while the woods provide some of the country's best-marked hiking trails.

Lake Placid has summer theater, concerts, and films. A pleasant day trip for Elderhostelers is offered to Whiteface Mountain with a very nice lunch served at the Saranac Inn. The hotel is owned by the college and used for hands-on training for students studying hotel and restaurant management.

Shortcomings: Paul Smith's Elderhostel program typifies a poor program run in a spectacular setting. Elderhostelers have no central lounge facilities for socializing, and the program is conducted by young, insensitive interns.

Getting In: "Easy. Just mail in your application."

Getting There: Attractive auto routes are available to the area. Interstate bus, feeder airline, and train are also possible, because Lake Placid is popular as both a summer and winter resort.

Potsdam—Clarkson University

Courses of Study: Biology of Local Farmland; Bach; American Short Story

Quality of Instructors: Good to excellent.

Environment: Clarkson has a beautiful, rambling campus and attractive modern buildings in northern New York State. This area of the St. Lawrence River Valley is truly remote. The nearest large city is Montreal, Quebec, 100 miles away. Artists and writers have immortalized the glories of the Adirondacks, the wildflowers, and sweet-scented balsam trees.

The village of Potsdam is a small paper manufacturing town of just 11,000 people. In addition to being the home of two universities, Clarkson and SUNY, it is the marketplace for all the neighboring towns and hamlets.

Housing: Excellent. Elderhostelers are housed in low brick buildings in rooms that have private baths. Clarkson wins an A-plus for cleanliness.

Food: The meals are very good and plentiful. A pleasant outdoor picnic and barbecue enhance the program.

Unique Attributes: The campus athletic facilities are excellent. The indoor swimming pool and tennis courts are available all day—no limitations on Elderhostel hours. The campus is fairly level and the buildings conveniently situated. The Elderhostel staff are considerate and hospitable and help to make this a favorite destination. Lake Placid nearby is a well-known winter and summer resort. The Lake Placid area, a tourist mecca, abounds with flea markets, antique fairs and craft shows in the spring, summer and fall. From Potsdam, one has a view of New York State's tallest peak— a mere 5,344 feet high.

Shortcomings: Do not forget the insect repellent for the six-week black fly season that ends in late June.

Getting In: Moderately difficult.

Getting There: Most people go by car along the Adirondack Northway, but there is a major airport in Montreal and some commuter flights to the Lake Placid area. Some public bus service is available.

North Carolina

Asheville—University of North Carolina at Asheville

Courses of Study: Thomas Wolfe; Western North Carolina History; Writing from Life

Quality of Instructors: Knowledgeable university professors pique the students' interest. Rated "very good."

Environment: The University of North Carolina at Asheville is a small, liberal arts college campus nestled between the Smoky Mountains and the Blue Ridge Parkway. The school combines the intimacy and friendliness characteristic of the South, and the charming town surrounding the campus epitomizes the grace and mores we associate with old-fashioned America. Asheville—gateway to the Parkway, a Cherokee Indian reservation, and the national park—has become a favorite tourist center. Its comfortable size (population 60,600), mountain location, and cool summer evenings draw many summer visitors.

Housing: Elderhosters stay in high-rise dormitories with semi-private rooms, four people sharing a bathroom. The buildings have elevators and air-conditioning, and lovely views of the mountains can be seen from the upper levels.

Food: Good North Carolina specialties are served—
ham, grits, and buttered biscuits.

Unique Attributes: One set of reviewers gave this program an A-plus. The visits to Thomas Wolfe's home
and cemetery, the evening at the theater, the extracurricular activities, and the picnic are all well planned
and executed. Some classes include interesting demonstrations of mountain music. Elderhostelers are kept
busy at all times and the management is always on
call.

The Smoky Mountain National Park straddles the border of Tennessee and North Carolina. This 522,000-
acre park is the most visited of all our national parks.
Mountain laurel the size of trees bloom from May
through July. Bus tours can be taken from Asheville to
the park. The city also has a botanic garden in which
one can view spectacular, tree-size azaleas and
rhododendrons. If you are in search of a touristy diversion, you might visit the Biltmore House and Gardens,
a 250-room mansion that was the elaborate home of
George Vanderbilt. This famous estate was designed to
replicate a French chateau.

Shortcomings: "None—everything's perfect," wrote
one pair of well-traveled Elderhostelers.

Getting In: This is a much-applauded program. Early
reservations are an absolute necessity.

Getting There: Asheville can be reached by public
bus, major air carriers, or private car. It has its own
very busy airport. If one wishes to tour Smoky Mountain National Park, a car is recommended.

Boone—Appalachian State University

Courses of Study: Southern Literature; Appalachian Music; Appalachian History; Nonverbal Communications; Values in Western Society

Quality of Instructors: Full professors of the university teach the Elderhostel courses. "In all my college work I never had better—give them an A-plus," wrote one much-traveled and much-educated hosteler. The course selection and content also received an A-plus rating from an Elderhostel fan.

Environment: This wonderful and most cordial 255-acre campus is part of the University of North Carolina system with an enrollment of 9,907 students. The town of Boone lies in the Blue Ridge Mountains and has gently rolling hills. It is a resort community situated 3,300 feet above sea level. "I recommend Appalachian State as a perfect introduction to Elderhosteling," wrote another Boone booster.

Housing: Elderhostelers stay in an elevator-equipped residence hall that is convenient to dining and classes. Even the parking is nearby.

Food: Elderhostelers dine in the school cafeteria with a particularly friendly group of students and are invited to eat as much as they wish.

Unique Attributes: The town of Boone offers scenic vistas of the Blue Ridge Parkway, where azaleas and dogwood turn the roadsides pink in the spring.

The school-sponsored field trips are well conducted and well designed for acquainting Elderhostelers with the lovely countryside. The entire place—school, classrooms, dining hall, and outdoor classrooms—abound with a feeling of hospitality and congeniality. Appalachians are proud, rugged people living on rugged land where handcrafting skills are still admired. A drive into the country will reveal spinning wheels, musical instruments, cane chair seats, and fabrics—all handmade.

Shortcomings: "Nonexistent," wrote my Boone booster.

Getting In: Expect to be wait-listed here. The possibility of immediate acceptance is chancy.

Getting There: Boone can be reached by interstate bus or plane to Winston-Salem, but an automobile would be advantageous in the mountainous part of North Carolina.

Highlands—The Mountain Highlands Camp and Conference Center

Courses of Study: Appalachian Folk History; Natural History Explorations; Our Southern Highlands; Central American Conflict

Quality of Instructors: "Wonderful," said one attendee. They "bring a fresh focus to familiar subjects."

Environment: The camp, a year-round Unitarian-Universalist retreat, is situated on top of a 4,200-foot mountain. Despite the location the grounds are comfortable and cozy and the walking is easy. In the fall, the Smoky Mountains are a blaze of color, and the weather is perfect. Highlands, sixty miles southwest of Asheville, is one of the resort towns in the Smokies.

Housing: There are two types of accommodations: a lodge with dormitory rooms that sleep four or rustic but comfortable cabins. The cabins have front porches from which there are spectacular views of the Smokies.

Food: Three times a day, Elderhostelers are served food that is too good. "The best of any hostel," wrote one much-traveled correspondent. Traditional black-eyed peas are often on the menu.

Unique Attributes: The friendly people and cordial atmosphere have induced one of my correspondents to return to "The Mountain" four times. The performance of the local storyteller and folksinger was one of her favorite experiences. Appalachia is the home of defiant, industrious, independent people with a musical tradition of guitars, fiddles, banjos, dulcimers, and bluegrass bands. The people have a great love of place and strong regionalism.

Vans are available in Boone for trips on the Blue Ridge Parkway, a road that winds through mountains carpeted with evergreens that get bluer and bluer as they recede into the distance. The Smokies are famous for having more than one hundred varieties of trees, and rumor has it that one can hardly drive through the Great Smokies without seeing one or more bears.

Shortcomings: Rain gear and insect repellent are suggested for trips into the Smoky Mountains in the summer.

Getting In: After this enthusiastic review, you may have to gamble on a lottery to enroll in this program.

Getting There: Although private automobile is the preferred method of transportation, one can get to Highlands on an interstate bus. Asheville, sixty miles away, is the nearest airport.

Piedmont—University of North Carolina at Chapel Hill

Courses of Study: All That Jazz: History and Illustrations; All that Jazz: Performance Techniques Laboratory; All That Jazz: Performance Mediums

Quality of Instructors: "Super-excellent, give them five stars," wrote one music-loving couple.

Environment: Chapel Hill is a town of contrasts. It is a town with a special Southern quality. Its colonial gardens and tree-shaded streets are fragrant with magnolias and wisteria. Although this idyllic college town retains some vestiges of plantation psychology, the school's atmosphere is unexpectedly enlightened and cosmopolitan.

The university, one of the leading public universities in the country, is rightfully proud of its green, lush, attractive campus. All of this charm contrasts sharply with the Chapel Hill-Raleigh-Durham research triangle of contemporary high technology.

Housing: Elderhostelers stay in high-rise, air-conditioned dormitories, two people to a room with one bathroom shared by every pair of bedrooms. Dining, swimming, and parking are all located conveniently nearby.

Food: The cuisine offered in the college cafeteria is excellent. "Too much, too good," groaned one couple I met at another Elderhostel. "They stretched our self-control to the limit."

Unique Attributes: If you wish to revisit the twenties and thirties on a musical stroll down memory lane, this course is designed for you. You will survey ragtime, blues, instrumental jazz, big bands, bebop, modal, free, and fusion. You will hear some greats and play along, too! The "All That Jazz" program combines three courses presented through lectures, demonstrations, video, and records.

"The teaching is superb. Jim Kecht has a wonderful communications skill and can demonstrate his lectures with his trumpet, which he plays like Louie Armstrong!"

The university president is supportive of the Elderhostel program. The Student Union shows free films, and the town of Chapel Hill is a delight. Astronomy fans should not miss the Morehead Planetarium. Soften a reed for your old sax or licorice stick, loosen the valves on your brass trumpet, pack them tenderly and bring them along, so you can sit in with the Friday night jam session.

Shortcomings: "When the weather is pleasant, the half-mile walk from dorms to classrooms is wonderful, but in the dog days of summer it can feel like you are climbing Mt. Everest."

Getting In: Classes are always full, so early registration is essential. "Many students are second-time and third-time repeaters."

Getting There: Splendid bus, train, and airplane service is available to Chapel Hill.

Waynesville—Western Carolina University

Courses of Study: Gemstones, Identify and Learn; China; Drawing on the Right Side of the Brain; A New Way of Seeing; Witchcraft in Colonial America; Ghostly Tales

Quality of Instructors: The university professors and the graduate student assistants received compliments for their excellence.

Environment: This is an off-campus program conducted in a sylvan setting at the Waynesville Country Club. Waynesville is near Asheville, North Carolina, in the most scenic area of the state, between the Blue Ridge Parkway and the Great Smokies. The Blue Ridge Parkway, in spite of its name, is not a wide macadam thruway—it is a charming, winding road that meanders through the mountains, affording travelers wooded vistas in all seasons of the year. Take a leisurely drive in the spring to see the hills carpeted with pink azaleas and white dogwood.

Housing: The accommodations for this program are unusually luxurious for an Elderhostel. Attendees stay in rooms with private bath facilities at the Country Club.

Food: Meals are "waitress served." My reviewers found the quality and variety very good.

Unique Attributes: The beautiful, mountainous location is very special. The Elderhostel staff are helpful and courteous. The classes are conducted in a setting of natural beauty at a country club that is situated midway between the university campus and Asheville. The club has a lovely twenty-seven-hole golf course with rolling green fairways.

Shortcomings: No weaknesses in the program were reported. This destination is a favorite among our more sybaritic Elderhostelers. The physical plant and atmosphere appeal to individuals who prefer being waited on.

Getting In: The Waynesville Country Club program may be a sleeper. Much to my surprise, no one has reported long waiting lists.

Getting There: Waynesville can be reached by motor coach or by airplane to Asheville.

Ohio

Athens—Ohio University

Courses of Study: The Civil War Era; Live Young as Long as Possible

Quality of Instructors: A fine crew of teachers who animate both mind and body.

Environment: The school is located in a typical small university town in the rolling green hills of southeastern Ohio. The school is very proud of its tree-lined brick walkways and its location overlooking the Hocking River. Athens, though just a small community, comes alive at night with student activities. The surrounding area is rich farmland, woodland, and state parks.

Housing: Elderhostelers report the housing as adequate. The university dormitories have recently had a face-lift and been renovated.

Food: The bill of fare is abundant and delicious. The quantities are ample enough to satisfy appetites stimulated by strenuous exercise.

Unique Attributes: The gracious, sociable atmosphere creates harmony among the Elderhostel group.

Elderhostelers participate in a carefully supervised program of physical activity tailored to their individual needs. A daily hike is followed by aerobic exercises and instruction in a chosen sport—golf, tennis, or swimming. The school has bicycle paths, too.

This is a very athletic campus. The nine-hole golf course and aquatic center are right on the premises. There is an old swimming hole two miles away from the campus, and in winter there is much snow and great downhill and cross-country skiing. The theater, dance, and art departments of the university sponsor events and exhibits and invite guest performers to the campus. Nearby is Hocking Hills State Park, an extraordinary park with cliffs of a geologic wonder called Black Hand Sandstone. Rock shelters, small waterfalls, and hiking trails wander through the hemlocks and birch trees.

Shortcomings: No weaknesses reported.

Getting In: This program seems to appeal to a special breed of fitness aficionados.

Getting There: Athens can be reached by private car over turnpikes, interstate bus, or regularly scheduled airlines to the Athens airport.

Oregon

Ashland—Southern Oregon State College

Courses of Study: Mushrooms; Wildflowers; Shakespeare Festival; Contemporary Theater; Elizabethan Music; Forestry

Quality of Instructors: The instructors received rave reviews: "excellent," "fantastic," and "superb" were among the comments. Many instructors for Shakespeare courses are selected from among the Shakespeare Festival personnel, and the naturalists show great affection for their subjects.

Environment: Southern Oregon State College has been hosting Elderhostelers since 1980 and has developed an avid fan club. All of the evaluation questionnaires returned to me were dotted with exclamation points and superlatives. Ashland is a "gorgeous college town." It has lovely, turn-of-the-century homes, and the theater is excellent. The atmosphere of the college is friendly. There is no institutional feeling, and Elderhostelers are encouraged to stay for two weeks. "The atmosphere is conducive to making lifelong friends."

Housing: The dormitories are immaculately clean and comfortable, "better than average." Some stair climbing is necessary.

Food: One not-so-enthusiastic couple rated the meals "very good most of the time." Everyone else gave the cafeteria fare a grade of excellent or splendid. A special area of the dining room is reserved for use of the Elderhostelers, a cozy arrangement that is much appreciated by the single travelers.

Unique Attributes: Ashland is the home of the famous Shakespeare Festival that runs annually from July to Labor Day. "We saw Shakespearean theater performances as fine as Stratford!" wrote one couple from the East Coast.

Ashland's Elderhostel program offers one an opportunity to see top-flight theater. In addition to Shakespeare, modern plays and carefully selected classics are performed.

The quality of the total program is superb. The staff is attentive twenty-four hours a day. The campus is within walking distance of the town, where one can shop, visit the parks, and play tennis. Expert river pilots are available for souls brave enough to try whitewater rafting. Ashland has a very healthful climate. It is close to the mountains and to Medford, the fruit capital of Oregon.

Shortcomings: The following is indicative of the response of most reviewers. "We've attended three Elderhostels at Southern Oregon State and cannot find any weaknesses." A few attendees mentioned the stair-climbing and two reviewers were disappointed in the cafeteria cleanup system.

Getting In: Getting accepted at Ashland is very difficult because this is one of the country's most highly applauded destinations. Early applications are recommended even though the national registration department is probably forced to use a lottery system for filling these classes. One reviewer wrote, "After three visits I would gladly go there again and again."

Getting There: Transportation by private automobile is easy, because Ashland is not off the beaten path. If you arrive in Medford by plane or bus, the college usually sends its own vans to meet Elderhostelers. This is not only convenient but also establishes a cordial feeling. I have been advised that because of the undependability of plane arrival times at the Medford airport, the Elderhostel director is now suggesting that attendees try to share a taxi or limo from the airport to the college. The airport is frequently shrouded in fog, which can make landing something of an uncertain adventure.

Monmouth—Western Oregon State College

Courses of Study: Botany; Baroque Music; Alaskan Life and Culture; Winemaking; Music of Broadway; Mineral Resources

Quality of Instructors: A multifaceted group. "All held our attention and stirred our imagination."

Environment: Monmouth is a medium-sized university town cradled midway between the driftwood-littered Oregon coast and the Cascade Mountains. The school is located in the pastoral Williamette Valley, an agricultural and sheep-grazing area of the state. The campus boasts of having the tallest Christmas tree in the world.

Housing: Elderhostelers enjoy the luxury of private apartments in a modern dormitory building. Each apartment consists of a sitting-room study with picture windows and desks, a separate bedroom, a closet, and private bathroom. Some apartments, however, are on the third floor of a walk-up building.

Food: The food served in the cafeteria is reputed to be very bad. "Barely edible," was the disdainful comment of one pair of roommates.

Unique Attributes: Western Oregon State College runs a perfectly organized program. The woman in charge is right on top of her task from the first evening orientation program until the party on the final night. The materials distributed at check-in are informative, clear, and helpful.

There is a small museum on the campus named and dedicated to Dr. Paul Jensen, a man who has spent twenty-four years living among the Eskimos. The hands-on Elderhostel classes are conducted in the museum by Dr. Jensen himself. The collection of artifacts is unique and fascinating. The Elderhostel evening programs are very entertaining; there is a box supper on the lawn, a folk-dancing display, a slide show, and a concert. One gentleman, a former Northeast urbanite, observed, "The natives pronounce the

name of their state as Orry-gun, Orry-g'n, or Organ.
Never Aura-gahn, the way we outlanders do."

Shortcomings: The poor quality of meals served in
the cafeteria seems to be this program's only weakness.

Getting In: No registration problems were reported
to me.

Getting There: The automobile drive to Monmouth is
over lovely winding roads. Salem, Oregon—a short distance from Monmouth—can be reached by plane, train,
or bus.

Sandy—Alton Collins Retreat Center

Courses of Study: Astronomy; Music; Art; In Search
of the True Amadeus; Life Cycles in the Forest; Whales
of the World

Quality of Instructors: All of the teachers, scholars,
and naturalists were rated as excellent.

Environment: Alton Collins is an adult education center in the Oregon rain forest. It is set in the snow-
covered Cascade Mountains amid mountain hemlock
and silver fir trees. Elderhostelers can stroll over lava
beds created by thousands of years of eruptions and
hike over trails gutted with cracks and crevasses.

Housing: The sleeping accommodations are superior.

Elderhostelers are housed in carpeted, double-occupancy bedrooms with private bathrooms.

Food: The meals at Alton Collins are graded as superior. "Home-type gourmet" meals are served family style at large round tables that encourage congeniality.

Unique Attributes: The accommodations and surroundings are splendid. The camp is surrounded by hiking trails through Oregon's tall timber of red cedar and maple. The program's highlight is a field trip to majestic Mt. Hood, the dormant volcano that's 11,245 feet high and has glacier-clad slopes. Elderhostelers gain a profound understanding of the word *scenic*—"we didn't go sightseeing, we lived it."

The people of Oregon are like their state—open, friendly, and outdoors-oriented. No overcrowding, smog, and slums in this state. Plan to go in June if you wish to visit Portland's highly regarded Rose Festival. Portland also boasts a five-and-a-half-acre Japanese garden that is open year-round. Sandy lies just thirty-five miles southeast of Portland.

Shortcomings: One needs an automobile to thoroughly enjoy the experience.

Getting In: This seems to be a rather popular program. Some of my reviewers wrote about waiting lists for acceptance. Early registrations are recommended.

Getting There: Portland can be reached by interstate bus, airplane, and train, although a leisurely drive up the driftwood-littered Oregon coast is recommended as the preferred method of transportation.

Pennsylvania

Bucks County—George School

Courses of Study: Field Botany; Quakerism; Swimming/Hydro-Therapy; Sound, Music, Light: Physics of Waves in Everyday Experience

Quality of Instructors: Academicians given an "excellent" and the specialists a "mediocre."

Environment: The coeducational, secondary Friends boarding school has a lovely campus full of towering mature trees. The school is affiliated with Pennswood Village, a life-care community also managed by the Quakers.

Pennsylvania is the Quaker state and Bucks is one of its most historic counties. This fertile valley on the Delaware River once harbored dairy and poultry farms and mule-drawn barges along its canal; nowadays, the town of New Hope has become a tourist mecca and the lovely farms converted into townhouse developments. There are Quaker meeting houses still in use, and the predominant architecture is slate-roofed, gray, Pennsylvania fieldstone.

Housing: Good to fair. Most rooms rather small for two people. The school provides fans!

Food: Good. Do not forget to try Philadelphia scrapple and cheesesteaks.

Unique Attributes: A wonderful opportunity to learn about Quakerism at the source and to visit Pennswood, the much-admired retirement community.

With a private car, Philadelphia is within reach. The city is celebrated for the Philadelphia Museum of Art, Fels Planetarium, Rodin Sculpture Museum, and outdoor summer orchestra concerts in the Dell. Bucks County has one of the country's oldest summer theaters and a good historical museum that houses a fine exhibit of Pennsylvania arts and crafts.

Shortcomings: The reviewers of this program were very disappointed not to dine regularly at Pennswood as promised in the catalog. They visited Pennswood and were very favorably impressed with the facility but regretted the misprint. If, for you, part of the program's inducement is the opportunity to take your evening meals at Pennswood, check before registering.

Getting In: No special difficulties.

Getting There: A private car is necessary if you wish to sightsee the tourist spots. The railroad station in Trenton, New Jersey, is the nearest Amtrak station, but New Hope is a commuter stop on the Reading Railroad. The Philadelphia airport is a long haul away over high-speed expressways.

Rhode Island

Providence—Johnson and Wales College

Courses of Study: Food Preparation; Nutrition

Instructors: Culinary artists and excellent nutritionists.

Environment: Providence is a spacious city, the capital of Rhode Island. Its location offers easy access to Boston. Johnson and Wales is a private, career-oriented school with an enrollment of 5,151 students, many of whom study food and hotel management. The school is known as "America's Hospitality College."

Housing: Elderhostelers are housed in a former hotel in private rooms with private baths. The air-conditioned building is now furnished in dormitory style.

Food: As one might expect, in addition to the very good regular meals, class participants sample all the dishes prepared in the classroom demonstrations. "Plenty to eat."

Unique Attributes: The gourmet-style menu and air-conditioned lodgings are superior to many other host institutions in Elderhosteling. Providence offers many cultural, educational, and recreational opportunities, and the Elderhostel management makes good use of these. Extracurricular activities include a visit to the Victorian Newport mansions, a sampling at a vineyard and winery, and an evening at the Providence theater (extra cost).

This program attracts a very congenial group of gourmands and gastronomes, hostelers who enjoy vegetable-carving contests as well as "bake- offs." The college owns two hotel complexes, the Rhode Island Inn and the Johnson & Wales Inn.

Shortcomings: Johnson and Wales has inadequate lounge areas for hostelers to enjoy after-class socializing. The field trips are made in non-air-conditioned buses, which can be miserable during a heat spell.

Getting In: My reviewers were accepted on the first try.

Getting There: Providence is an easy drive from any East Coast city. It is the gateway for a motor tour of Cape Cod, Plymouth, Boston, and the islands of Nantucket and Martha's Vineyard. Providence is also a major transportation center, served by airplane, bus, or train.

South Dakota

Yankton—Mount Marty College

Courses of Study: Indian Culture; Calligraphy; Tales of the Old West

Quality of Instructors: Very good. The instructors cast old ideas in a new light.

Environment: Yankton is a city in the southeast corner of South Dakota on the Nebraska border overlooking Lewis and Clark Lake. South Dakota is famous for windswept prairies and extremes of unpleasant weather—dust storms in the summer and heavy snow in the winter. Mount Marty is a small Catholic coed college with an enrollment of 620 students. It is a Benedictine institution with a nice rolling campus.

Housing: Elderhostelers stay in very clean, neat, two-person dormitory rooms. The bedrooms have their own washbasins and the toilet and tub bathrooms each serve a pair of bedrooms.

Food: The meals are satisfactory.

Unique Attributes: The Benedictine Sisters who direct the Elderhostel program work very hard to make the attendees' stay pleasant and comfortable. The well-planned extracurricular field trips include a delightful midsummer Swedish Festival and an Indian mission, and the evening entertainment includes a great demonstration by a folk and square dance group, all of whom are over age sixty-five.

South Dakota has many wonderful sight-seeing attractions: the barren canyons of the Badlands, pre-historic fossils, the ancient Black Hills where gold was discovered, and the Mount Rushmore Memorial with the heads of four great Americans carved in granite.

Shortcomings: Some individuals might be nettled by the lack of shower facilities.

Getting In: My reviewers were registered on their first try.

Getting There: My reviewers flew to Omaha and rented a car for the drive to Yankton. The airports at Sioux Falls, South Dakota, and Sioux City, Iowa, are closer to Yankton and equally convenient for touring South Dakota before or after the week of school.

Tennessee

Paris Landing State Resort Park in Buchanan, Tennessee—Austin Peay State University of Clarksville

Courses of Study: Civil War Battles of Fort Donelson; Myths and Beliefs in Rural Tennessee; Birds of the Area; The Constitution

Quality of Instructors: The very good professors from Austin Peay are assisted by local foresters and ornithologists, as required.

Environment: Paris Landing is a state-owned park located in the Land Between the Lakes Recreation Area, which includes two beautiful lakes and a wilderness area. A bird refuge and the national military park and cemetery at Fort Donelson are also part of this recreation complex set among green, rolling hills. The TVA dams form the most completely controlled river system in the world.

Housing: Elderhostelers are housed in a deluxe hotel owned and operated by the state of Tennessee. The modern hotel (its rooms have private baths) overlooks the man-made Kentucky Lake.

Food: Superb meals are served buffet style. Expect "down home" food in Tennessee.

Unique Attributes: The deluxe accommodations (not always found in Elderhostels) received many compliments. This program includes many particularly interesting field trips. The van takes Elderhostelers to the famous civil war battlefield at Fort Donelson, where General Simon Buckner surrendered to Ulysses S. Grant. Relics of the battle—sabers, muskets, trenches, and gun batteries—mark the North's first major victory in 1862. Elderhostelers also visit the Homestead, a model 1850 farm complete with live animals, spinning wheels, and weaving looms.

Birders have an opportunity to identify many varieties of cardinals and to spot wild turkeys and mockingbirds in the bird sanctuary.

Shortcomings: The university and park are forty-five miles apart. Although the Elderhostel administrators and teachers join the group for dinner at Paris Landing, several much-traveled Elderhostelers believe the distance has a negative impact on the program. The use of other university facilities is precluded and there is a lack of after-hours camaraderie with the faculty.

Getting In: The hotel is able to accommodate a fairly large group and has not to date been troubled with long waiting lists.

Getting There: Clarksville, Tennessee, can be reached by regularly scheduled flights, and there is public bus service to the park. If you wish to thoroughly explore the countryside before or after the program, my reviewers suggest traveling by private automobile.

Texas

Austin—St. Edwards University

Courses of Study: Computers; Texas History; Learning to Listen Creatively; Introduction to Hispanic Culture

Quality of Instructors: Top-notch professors who are effective communicators.

Environment: St. Edwards enjoys a great college environment in Austin. Austin is the state capital and locale of the largest university campus in Texas, the University of Texas. This university is so large that one dormitory complex has its own zip code. The land rolls gently and the horizon is far-reaching. Austin sits in the middle of the state and is a booming high-tech city but retains an old-fashioned, walkable downtown. The capitol itself is a red-granite version of the nation's capitol in D.C., with a lone star at the apex of the Texas dome. Cattle still graze on the outskirts of town.

Housing: Elderhostelers stay in comfortable, handsome dormitory rooms with semi-private bath and toilet facilities. The rooms are air-conditioned and singles are available.

Food: The university cafeteria provides delicious, filling meals—"classic college fare," I was told.

Unique Attributes: The Elderhostel director, Sister Madeline Sophie Weber, tends tirelessly to every need of the attendees. Texas oil money has made the University of Texas a prosperous institution and has made Austin a fast-growing metropolitan city. In response to huge student demands, Austin has film festivals, opera, traveling theater, and excellent museums. There are literary events, good bookstores, record stores, and funky cafes, all patronized by the students. Austin also has an avant-garde music scene that plays both jazz and country.

Shortcomings: Texas can be hotter than the hinges of hell in the summer, but fortunately, all the buildings at St. Edwards are air-conditioned.

Getting In: St. Edwards University has been able to accommodate Elderhostel registration requests as received.

Getting There: Austin is a metropolitan city that has frequent service by major air carriers, buses, and trains.

Utah

Cedar City—Southern Utah State College

Courses of Study: Flora and Fauna; Geology of Southern Utah; Shakespearean Festival; The Life and Times of William Shakespeare

Quality of Instructors: "The teachers at Southern Utah are competent in their fields, witty, and have an easy, likable manner."

Environment: "The environment is exquisite." The school has a charming little campus set in the heart of town. "It's one of the cleanest, most wholesome places I've ever been." This is a pretty area of Utah, not all dust dry creek beds and sagebrush, as one might expect.

Housing: Elderhostelers stay in tiny but adequate rooms in an old-fashioned dormitory with communal bath and toilet facilities. The air-conditioned building is a three-flight walk-up.

Food: A small, nice cafeteria in the student center serves a cuisine that is "the best of many Elderhostels."

Unique Attributes: Cedar City is the home of the renowned Utah Shakespeare Festival. Student productions of Shakespeare are presented in the evening in an outdoor theater designed to replicate the Globe Theater in England. There is also an indoor theater for use in inclement weather. "A beautifully costumed, well-rehearsed cast perform on handsomely designed sets," wrote the reviewer. Each evening performance is preceded by a daily morning seminar and an evening pre-curtain lecture on the current production. Tickets for three performances are included in the Elderhostel registration fee.

The Elderhostel program also includes a day trip to two splendid national parks. They visit the monoliths of Zion National Park with its natural arches, mesas, and buttes striated in red and pink, as well as the great stone pinnacles and horseshoe-shaped amphitheaters of Bryce Canyon.

Shortcomings: The weather in southern Utah can be very wet in August. Apparently the indoor theater is used frequently. My panelist reported that in his opinion the students performed with "mediocre proficiency." This was a drawback but not serious enough to keep him from reenrolling at this destination.

Getting In: In spite of all the accolades, the Cedar City Shakespeare Festival is not as well known as the Oregon Festival. My reviewers experienced no difficulty in registering for the program.

Getting There: Cedar City can be reached by interstate bus or by a commuter airline from Phoenix, Arizona.

Provo—Brigham Young University

Courses of Study: Genealogy Workshop; Composing Your Personal History; Genealogy Library Workshop

Quality of Instructors: The Mormon professors are very serious about education and have a somber approach to marriage, child-rearing, and family. All teachers are very proficient.

Environment: Brigham Young University is owned and operated by the Church of the Latter Day Saints, whose tenets create a pleasant but very conservative atmosphere. The university has a code of honor, a dress code that prohibits the wearing of shorts, and a prohibition against caffeine and alcohol. Even the students' hair length is regulated—the boys may not wear pony tails.

The absence of student cafes makes Provo very quiet at night, but the cleanliness and well-tended landscape of the town and campus make for a very pleasant quality of life. Brigham Young has an attractive suburban campus that spreads along the shores of the freshwater Utah Lake.

Housing: The dormitories, like the rest of the campus, are spotlessly clean. There are central television rooms and swimming pools right in the sex-segregated dormitories.

Food: The meals are wonderful—lots of homemade breads and delectable homemade ice cream. At Brigham Young the groaning board really groans. The invention of caffeine-free cola was met with great eagerness at Brigham Young.

Unique Attributes: The largest library on the subject of genealogy is the Mormon Library in Salt Lake City. Although Provo does not swing like many university towns at night, the school has its own symphony, an active drama department, fine cinema, and a jazz group. All sporting events are well attended. Because of the Mormon belief in education, Utah boasts a uniquely high percentage of high school and college graduates. Every Elderhostel day opens with an inter-denominational prayer—"a nice touch, not offensive to anyone," said one of my panelists. The automobile drive to Provo takes one over steep switchbacks, past cobalt-blue lakes, stone arches, and natural bridges.

Shortcomings: The Elderhostel program at Brigham Young is top-notch in every respect.

Getting In: I would have expected to hear complaints about long waiting lists for this destination, but no such reports were forwarded to me.

Getting There: Provo has good interstate bus service and can be reached by connecting airplane flights from Salt Lake City.

Salt Lake City—University of Utah

Courses of Study: Family Relations in Cross-Cultural Perspective; Hitler and Nazi Germany; Folklife in Utah; The Search for Alexander the Great; The Failure of a Dream; The Five Faces of the Middle East; The Eye of the Beholder

Quality of Instructors: The courses are taught by a group of very competent university professors; "excellent lecturers."

Environment: This Mormon university straddles both the capital city of Utah and the Wasatch Mountains. The many old buildings of the school are nestled on the side of a mountain overlooking the city. This is an urban school; 75 percent of its 25,000 students are commuters. The atmosphere is cosmopolitan, very different from the campus of small, self-contained suburban schools. The fifteen-hundred-acre campus of the university includes museums, libraries, and an arboretum that boasts an exhibition of 300 varieties of trees. The student body is a relatively clean-cut, clean-shaven group. In Salt Lake City, alcoholic beverages are served only in private clubs. The weather is splendid—clear and dry because of the altitude.

Housing: The dormitories are well maintained and comfortable.

Food: The meals served in the student union cafeteria are very good. The cafeteria has beautifully decorated eating and lounging areas, designed to encourage the commuter-students not to hurry home. Nibbles are always available, so the hall is used for students to hang out, talk, and snack.

Unique Attributes: Salt Lake City is a gracious city with wide avenues, beautiful Mormon Church buildings, and monuments. It is a thriving cultural center, with an opera company, a symphony orchestra, dance companies with national reputations, an opulent theater, and, of course, the famous Mormon Tabernacle Choir. The Museum of Natural History has a unique exhibit of fossils and dinosaurs. Salt Lake City offers the visitor an opportunity to take a sunset cruise, tour strange-colored gorges and canyons, and swim in the clean, salty water of the Great Salt Lake, where swimmers are unsinkable. The Mormon strictures are pervasive at the University of Utah, but because most of the students are commuters, the atmosphere is more relaxed than at Brigham Young.

Shortcomings: Really vigorous walking is required by the Elderhostelers since the housing, meals and classes are very far apart, and the hills to be climbed are steep. I must caution readers that one hosteler reported a very regrettable experience at this university. An inefficient hostess made little or no evening plans, relied solely on participants' private cars for in-town transportation, and in brief, was rarely in evidence. The cafeteria eating was disorganized, the school too large and unfriendly, and the single travelers were just "lost in the shuffle."

Getting In: My reviewers did not report any problems.

Getting There: Salt Lake City is a transportation center with an international airport, a bus terminal, and a train depot that receives passenger service of Amtrak's California Zephyr.

Vermont

Poultney—Green Mountain College

Courses of Study: Robert Frost, Vermont's Poet Laureate; Elementary Drawing; Wildflowers of Vermont

Quality of Instructors: Reports ranged from very good to gifted and outstanding.

Environment: Poultney is a quaint New England town located on the New York-Vermont border, twenty miles southwest of Rutland. Poultney is in the midst of some major ski areas, Killington, Stratton and Bromley. The mountainous countryside is beautiful in all seasons, green and lush in the summer, ablaze in brilliant color in the fall, and a still blanket of whiteness in the winter.

Green Mountain College has a 155-acre campus. Its modern facilities include an art center with studios, a television and audiovisual lab, and a physical education complex of swimming pool and dance studios. Green Mountain is a very small coed school of 350 men and women. Its buildings are in the classic New England college style.

Housing: This small school has six residence halls. Elderhostelers stay in twin-bedded dormitory rooms with communal bath facilities. There are alternate floors for men and women and single rooms are available.

Food: The menu is ample, and the quality of food served is satisfactory. My reviewers complimented the cafeteria staff for their very nice variety of salads.

Unique Attributes: The quality of courses offered at the Green Mountain College program received accolades from my panelists. Particular note was made of the teacher who brought the Frost poetry course to life and the wildflower walks in local fields and meadows. This program can put you in touch with nature, people, and ideas. The extracurricular activities are very good. They include a picnic and swim at a nearby state park and lake and an outdoor barbecue on campus. In Rutland, the Norman Rockwell Museum, with 2,000 pieces of Rockwell memorabilia, is worth visiting. One couple recommended a stop at the Calvin Coolidge home and museum.

Shortcomings: None noted.

Getting In: My panelists were accepted on the first try.

Getting There: Poultney is situated on excellent interstate highways and has an Amtrak railroad station. Rutland is the nearest airport.

Virginia

Staunton—Mary Baldwin College

Courses of Study: The South; Creative Writing

Quality of Instructors: The professors are very good, skillful communicators.

Environment: The college has a beautiful campus spread on a hillside overlooking the historic Shenandoah Valley. Staunton is a city of 25,000 people whose Southern lifestyle is more leisurely and more hospitable than their neighbors to the north. The predominant architectural style of Staunton is a European classic design that uses local materials of red brick and painted wood. Virginia has a countrified grandeur, and its residents seem to have a pride and deep sense of our country's valuable heritage.

Housing: The dormitories are very clean and well equipped.

Food: One Elderhosteler with a low threshold of culinary resistance complained that the meals at Mary Baldwin are too enticing. "Nothing ordinary about this college fare," she said.

Unique Attributes: Staunton is ideally located for visiting historic shrines and for enjoying a national park. It is near Charlottesville, the Harding birthplace, and Monticello, the home of Thomas Jefferson. The countryside is dotted with memorials to great men and great Civil War battles. The Skyline Drive runs along the top of mountain ridges of the Shenandoah National Park and the Blue Ridge Parkway (the most scenic drive of the south), then meanders past Virginia's Natural Bridge. One Elderhosteler commented that her visit to the roots of democracy "strengthened her awareness of the ideas and forces that promoted freedom in the past."

Shortcomings: The campus is very hilly, difficult going for people whose walking ability is limited. The opportunities for sightseeing are wonderful—but that means taking your own wheels to the campus.

Getting In: In spite of Staunton's proximity to all the East Coast megalopolises, none of my reviewers complained about long waiting lists for this program.

Getting There: If one has the time and energy for a heavy dose of American history, an automobile is the preferred method of getting to Mary Baldwin. If not, Staunton can be reached by Trailways or Greyhound bus, Amtrak, or Piedmont Airlines.

Washington

Ellensburg—Central Washington University

Courses of Study: Astronomy; Mythology and Folklore; The Big Band Era

Quality of Instructors: The teaching staff are excellent communicators.

Environment: Central Washington University is a coed, state-supported institution of sixty-three hundred undergraduates. The spacious, beautiful campus is spread along the Yakima River surrounded by mountains. The Kittitas Valley is a high green valley nestled between mountains and desert.

The area is dotted with alpine lakes and apple orchards, the winters are white and cold, and the air is free of pollution. Central Washington is filled with stands of Douglas firs, ancient forests that are valuable as lumber as well as wilderness areas. Washington is aptly named the Evergreen State.

Housing: Accommodations are in a conference center that has both single and double rooms.

Food: The university cafeteria is better than most. Elderhostelers enjoy lots of fresh berries and local apples served in a variety of recipes.

Unique Attributes: The Elderhostel program administration gets a rating of five stars. The director is a young woman with a Master's degree in recreation, and, according to my reviewers, she must have earned all As in her courses. The boat trip, field trips, and evening activities are planned and executed in an exemplary fashion. All field trips are included in the cost of tuition. The music professor has his own "big band" and illustrates his lectures with records and lots of great live music.

Shortcomings: None, unless one has difficulty with the extensive amount of walking required.

Getting In: My reviewers said that Ellensburg is their favorite of fourteen Elderhostels attended. If it is not popular yet, I wager that it soon will be.

Getting There: The nearest airport is Spokane, but I have heard that the drive over Snoqualmie Pass is especially beautiful and well worth the effort.

Packwood—Lower Columbia College

Courses of Study: Mount Ranier: Past and Present

Quality of Instructors: A very good husband and wife team; he is a physical education teacher and she is a botany instructor. Members of the Forest Service staff add lectures, demonstrations, and field trips to the college faculty lectures.

Environment: Packwood is a small lumbering town seventy-five miles north of Portland, Oregon, in the foothills of Mount Ranier. It is a superbly scenic area. The town is located just a few miles from the entrance to the beautiful mountains of the national park.

Housing: Elderhostelers stay in the Royal Inn Motel in Packwood. No singles are available, but all rooms have private baths. The motel amenities include an indoor pool, cable TV, and telephones.

Food: Poor. Breakfast and dinner are served in a local restaurant with a fixed menu and no choices. Some meals are unappetizing and meager. Lunches are served picnic style—sandwiches and fruit are eaten in picnic areas of the park. "On the last night, a very good outdoor salmon bake was hosted by the instructors at their nearby home."

Unique Attributes: The whole week is spent hiking and exploring the magnificence of the 14,410-foot-high Mount Ranier. The mountain, which seems to hover over Seattle, still has gassy fumes spewing out of its volcanic cone. Wildflowers edge the glaciers, and dense forests of cedars and fir cover the south slope.

Shortcomings: My reviewers were unhappy with the accommodations. The bedrooms are very small and lack drawer space for the storage of clothing. The proprietors provided milk cartons, but attendees must primarily live out of their suitcases.

Getting In: No problems reported. My reviewers were accepted on the first try.

Getting There: Packwood can be reached by bus, plane or train. One can fly to San Francisco or Portland and rent a car for an interesting drive visiting Mt. St. Helens, the Columbia River Gorge, Crater Lake, and Lake Tahoe.

Seattle—Seattle University

Courses of Study: Russia (Myths and Truths); The Reticent Canadian; History of Japan; The Shadow of Beethoven

Quality of Instructors: Extremely well-qualified, good-humored professors with pleasant personalities.

Environment: The university has an urban campus right in the heart of Seattle, but the atmosphere is so conducive to scholarly pursuits that the city does not intrude on the Elderhostel program. The city enjoys a mild maritime climate, albeit cloudy and rainy, and has a manageable downtown district, replete with bookstores, art galleries, and jazz clubs. Seattle is a prosperous city, a condition that had its beginnings in the Klondike Gold Rush of the 1890s. Some historic artifacts of the period can be found in the city's museums. The climate during the summer is perfect; it stays light until 10 p.m., and the gardens and flowers are lush. Seattle tends to be cloudy, but the amount of rainfall is exaggerated. Seattle University is a Jesuit school on a clean, beautiful, forty-one-acre campus that is within walking distance of the Puget Sound waterfront.

Housing: Elderhostelers are usually housed in a large, modern dormitory, alternating floors with college students and people enrolled in other programs. The bathroom facilities seem inadequate when the dormitories are fully occupied.

Food: Excellent food is served in abundance in the school cafeteria. Once again I heard the same old lament—"too much, too good." While in Seattle, you will be served lots of small, crisp, locally grown apples, reminiscent of the fruit of your childhood, as well as plenty of fresh fish.

Unique Attributes: The dormitory is in a lovely building that also has a very large lobby with comfortable social group seating. Each floor has a small television and "nibble" room with coffee, tea and cookies available at all hours. The dining room is also in the same building. The school is conveniently located within walking distance of beautiful shopping arcades and right on a public bus route to the downtown area. The city has a passion for parks; in the spring the blooming Japanese cherry trees rival those in Washington, D.C. There is also a famous farmers' market with fishmongers and flower stalls. The Elderhostel staff is attentive and well prepared, and the program is well balanced. One couple attended a session when the campus was deserted except for the Elderhostelers. They found the experience pleasant.

Shortcomings: Some reviewers believed the bathroom facilities inadequate for the number of people in the program. "Otherwise, everything's perfect."

Getting In: During the year of the Expo, Seattle was a much-in-demand destination with long waiting lists. Since that time no difficulties have been encountered.

Getting There: Seattle is a major city easily reached by all forms of public transportation.

Wisconsin

Ashland—Northland College

Courses of Study: Birds Around the Bay; Weatherwise or Otherwise?; Woods and Wetlands of the North; Reading the Northern Landscape

Quality of Instructors: A dynamic group of professors of wildlife management and environmental studies.

Environment: Ashland is located on Chequamegon Bay, a bustling port on Lake Superior, and the campus is just one mile away. Chequamegon Bay, according to legend, is the "Shining Big Sea Water" of Longfellow's epic poem, "Hiawatha." Wisconsin is a favorite vacationland. Its glistening lakes and streams, hundreds of waterfalls, hardwood forests, and cool summer weather are great attractions. Wisconsin lies on the path of the Mississippi flyway, and flocks of birds migrate in the spring and fall, while herds of Guernseys graze in the meadows.

Housing: Elderhostelers are housed in usual college dormitories.

Food: Satisfactory.

Unique Attributes: Northland is a small school founded to bring higher education to isolated logging camps and farm communities. Elderhostelers enjoy swimming in the refreshing waters of Lake Superior and watching the fishermen trolling. On campus is the Sigurd Olson Environmental Institute in an earth-sheltered, solar-heated building. "A good mix," wrote one reviewer. Elderhostelers take field trips into woods and swamps and to historic Madeline Island. The twenty-three glacier-created Apostle Islands are clustered in the cold waters of Lake Superior. Madeline Island, with lovely, soft sand beaches on the sheltered side, is one of these twenty-three beautiful islands. Bring your binoculars along with your inquiring mind.

Shortcomings: Summer is short and the winters vigorous in Wisconsin.

Getting In: I am not aware of any registration difficulties at this destination.

Getting There: Ashland is serviced by the Duluth, Minnesota/Superior, Wisconsin, airport.

Milwaukee—Mt. Mary

Courses of Study: Innovators, Mystics, and Martyrs in Drama; Food for Thought—Eat, Drink, and Be Wary; Societal Perspectives: Caribbean, Alaska, Soviet Union

Quality of Instructors: "Both kites and ideas fly at Mt. Mary." The school is directed by the Sisters of Notre Dame, an order proud of its tradition of teaching excellence.

Environment: Mt. Mary is an urban campus right on the Menomonee River Parkway in a residential area of Milwaukee, five minutes from a shopping mall and fifteen minutes from downtown. It is a Catholic school for women, and its Tudor-Gothic buildings are all located on a level campus in close proximity to one another. The city of Milwaukee is the center of German-American culture in the United States and is also the beer capital of the country. Beer gardens, beer steins, and lederhosen give the city its special local color. "Gemutlichkeit" best describes the city's convivial atmosphere.

The city covers ninety-six square miles on the western shore of Lake Michigan, and its harbor is the chief port on the Great Lakes. The opening of the St. Lawrence Seaway made Milwaukee a major seaport with docks and piers and large oceangoing vessels.

Housing: The dormitories have double or single rooms with one washroom to serve each pair.

Food: Elderhostelers are offered three meals a day in the usual college cafeteria steam-table style.

Unique Attributes: The college's location permits easy access to downtown Milwaukee by public transportation—"If you can find the time," my reviewer wrote. Milwaukee has many diversions, legitimate theater, symphony concerts, a ballet company, and beautiful churches. It also boasts a lakefront art museum. One can also "do" the city on a sight-seeing Gray Bus Line. This is a particularly comfortable destination for hostelers who do not travel by private automobile. The college promotes physical fitness with a fitness center, four tennis courts, jogging and bike paths, and cross-country ski trails for winter use.

Shortcomings: No weaknesses reported.

Getting In: No problems reported.

Getting There: Milwaukee is a major transportation center. One can get there by wheels or wings.

Sheboygan—Lakeland College

Courses of Study: Philosophy; It's Never too Late to Learn German; German Culture; Discovering the Artist Within You

Quality of Instructors: Excellent. They demonstrate a genuine concern for students and subject matter.

Environment: Small Lakeland College, with its twelve hundred students, has a rural tranquillity and a bucolic country atmosphere. The campus lies one hour's drive north of Milwaukee and ten miles north of Sheboygan. The school is near both lakes and forests: Lake Michigan, Elkhart Lake, and the Kettle Moraine State Forest. Sheboygan is a popular fishing port on the western shore of Lake Michigan.

Housing: In modern residence halls that are convenient to both the classrooms and dining hall.

Food: Typical college fare is offered. One Elderhosteler, a woman weary of her domestic duties, wrote, "As long as I'm not cooking, it's all good." Sheboygan celebrates an annual event known as "Bratwurst Day," so I would not be suprised if the "wurst" in Sheboygan must be the best!

Unique Attributes: Milwaukee is the center of German-American culture in the United States, and some of this spills over into Sheboygan and Lakeland College. While dairy cattle graze on the Wisconsin plains, the factories are busy pressing cheese and the breweries concocting beer. The state is a sportsman's paradise: sparkling lakes are full of muskellunge, pike, and bass for the fisherman, hunters chase the deer, and the really intrepid go iceboating on Lake Michigan. Nearby Kohler Village has lovely landscaped gardens and the Kohler Arts Center mounts exhibitions, dance recitals, and concerts.

Shortcomings: My reviewers complained about the poor recreational facilities at the college. "No swimming pool—walking our only choice."

Getting In: At this time the Lakeland College program is not hampered by waiting lists.

Getting There: Milwaukee is served by most major air carriers and interstate railroad lines. Sheboygan is on the interstate bus routes.

Treehaven—University of Wisconsin, Stevens Point

Courses of Study: Field Study of Our Northern Birds

Quality of Instructors: An excellent group of birders and regional experts in the field of ornithology.

Environment: A beautiful, wooded, 1,000-acre site full of birds, birds, and birds. Treehaven is a fully winterized natural resource educational facility of the University of Wisconsin, not far from Rhinelander.

Housing: Good, dormitory-style facilities with shared baths. Singles are available, and women are on one floor and men on another. "Dorms coed from 11 p.m. to 5 a.m.—worked fine."

Food: Good and plentiful. Nice cookouts and picnics on field trips.

Unique Attributes: Eager bird watchers turn out for voluntary 6 a.m. bird walks. The staff are very adept at hearing, identifying, and locating birds, and they conduct field trips to nearby areas in search of different species. Indoor classes are combined with outdoor excursions, and guest speakers present evening programs. This is a fulfilling adventure that keeps one in touch with nature and people. Remember your binoculars. In Rhinelander one can see an old-time lumbering display, complete with a working narrow-gauge railroad locomotive.

Shortcomings: None.

Getting In: No problem; reviewer was admitted on the first try.

Getting There: "Treehaven is an easy drive over nice highways through beautiful country." Northwest and United airlines fly to Rhinelander, and the staff make arrangements to meet your plane.

Whitewater—University of Wisconsin at Whitewater

Courses of Study: Madame Bovary; Let's Go on with the Show: Favorite Musical Hits; Micros=Macs=Magic; Bicentennial of the U.S. Constitution

Quality of Instructors: A particularly competent and caring group of instructors.

Environment: Whitewater is in southern Wisconsin between the state's two largest cities, Milwaukee and Madison. The university campus sits on the edge of the Kettle Moraine State Forest, 18,000 acres of rough, wooded country. The buildings are spread over gentle green hills near lakes teeming with game fish, while many varieties of violets, the state flower, can be found in the woods. The university is one of the the Big Ten. Cold blasts of Canadian air often blow across Lake Michigan and bring frost and snow to Wisconsin in early October.

Housing: Elderhostelers sleep in student dormitories with communal bath facilities.

Food: The meals served at the Whitewater program are judged to be somewhat too institutional. The classic college fare needs some imaginative touches to earn higher grades from the Elderhostelers.

Unique Attributes: Because of its geographic isolation, a very pleasant sense of camaraderie exists at Whitewater. Another factor that encourages the friendly atmosphere is the informal dialogue that transpires when the professors dine with the Elderhostelers. One of the program highlights is an early evening cruise on Lake Geneva, a resort area famous for its palatial shoreline estates. Sheboygan, like much of Wisconsin, has beer gardens that vibrate with music and fun after the sun goes down.

Shortcomings: The physical facilities are not as comfortable as many Elderhostel destinations. The dining room is some distance from the dormitory and up a flight of steps. The lack of air-conditioning in the dormitories can be troublesome during the summer months.

Getting In: No problems were reported in any Wisconsin programs.

Getting There: Madison is the nearest major travel center, and it has excellent service by air, interstate bus, or train.

International Programs

Elderhostel conducts many of its international programs in conjunction with a "partner," travel organiza-
tions such as Saga, The Experiment in International
Living, or IST, the International Study Tours. Despite
this arrangement, Elderhostel remains an educational
program, and participants are expected to attend
classes and lectures much as they do at host institutions in the United States. The courses given abroad
are not for credit, nor is homework assigned, but the
emphasis is on study—not on sight-seeing.

Group travel arrangements are made for most destinations. The price of Elderhostel international programs
usually includes round-trip airfare on regularly scheduled airlines; all within-country travel; full room and
board; course-related excursions and admission fees;
and limited accident, sickness, and baggage insurance.

The Elderhostel programs in Israel, Brazil, Egypt,
France, and Greece are under the auspices of IST. International Study Tours is an organization, established in
Massachusetts in 1981, that offers two- and three-
week programs at twenty major universities and academic institutions on four continents.

 Saga Holidays, Ltd. is an English company with
thirty-five years of experience in serving the vacation

needs of British pensioners over sixty years old. Saga programs have an educational focus and feature classes in England, Scotland, Wales, and the Republic of Ireland.

The Experiment in International Living is a worldwide, not-for-profit federation that has been offering homestay vacations for students since 1932. Organized to improve international understanding on a personal level, their services now include United Nations projects and homestay programs for seniors in fifty nations. In 1988, Elderhostel/Experiment in International Living jointly sponsored programs in France, India, Switzerland, West Germany, Mexico, and Japan.

Elderhostel programs in China (American Huajia Study) are organized in cooperation with CAEE, a nonprofit organization based at the College of Staten Island of the City University of New York in conjunction with Chinese universities. CAEE has been offering university and professional exchange programs with China since 1979. Although Elderhostelers are treated as distinguished guests, the three-week study programs—through lectures, on-site visits, and informal dialogues with instructors, students, and Chinese families—permit participants to observe China as friends and students, not as mere visitors.

Some programs in Scandinavia and a half dozen northern European countries are conducted under the auspices of Scandinavian Seminars, Inc., an organization that since 1949 has been providing opportunities for American college students to spend a year of living and learning in Scandinavia. The Elderhostelers spend three weeks of travel and study with daily lectures in English.

All international opportunities are more thoroughly described in the official Elderhostel catalog than are domestic destinations. Therefore, I have included here a mere sampling of some selected sites to give a sense of hosteling around the world—an experience as original and impossible to categorize as are the domestic programs.

Bermuda

St. George—Bermuda Biological Station

Courses of Study: Bermuda's Delicate Balance: Introduction to Marine Science; Atlantic Coral Reefs; Bermuda's Historical/Architectural Heritage

Quality of Instructors: The program is taught by an accomplished group of technicists and marine scientists deeply concerned about the environment and the pollution in the Atlantic Ocean that is now poisoning their islands' beautiful sand beaches.

Environment: The biological station sits on the water's edge in a tropical park not far from St. George. The Bermuda chain of islands, a British Crown Colony, lies in the North Atlantic east of the Carolinas. St. George is one of the seven largest of the bridge-linked islands. Bermuda is a popular resort for U.S. citizens. Refugees from the cold as well as artists and writers seek the quiet warmth of the island sun, the clean air, and sounds of birdsong. The windswept islands offer a retreat into the past. Uniformed constables, carriages, bicycles, and the clatter of horses hooves are reminiscent of the nineteenth-century English countryside.

Housing: The sleeping accommodations for the program can vary. Hostelers may find themselves in the main hotel building or in cottages or apartments, but the bedrooms in all accommodations are unheated. The common areas at the station are heated when necessary by space heaters.

Food: The bill of fare is nutritious and delicious. A traditional English afternoon teatime is observed.

Unique Attributes: The Elderhostel program is scheduled from Monday afternoon through breakfast the following Sunday. My reviewer wrote, "I attended a one week Elderhostel that should have been stretched to two, so much was packed into each day." "Very strenuous program," another panelist commented. Bermuda's uniqueness is in its smallness and isolation, its pink sand beach, and its devotion to English traditions. Narrow lanes and alleys, bowered in pink oleanders, are enclosed by high stuccoed walls edged with pastel-colored morning glories. The early homes were built of hurricane-resistant, white-washed stone, and the architectural style remains unchanged. Clean, simple, comfortless, limestone block houses dot the landscape. Many of the old sounds and smells are still there, but the automobile and ocean pollution have destroyed some of the islands' quaint loveliness.

Fort St. Catherine is a nearby tourist attraction that dates from the early 1600s. Tourism brings problems, but it also brings excellent shopping opportunities. English goods, leather, knitwear, and fine china are available in both tiny and spacious gift shops.

Shortcomings: The winter weather in Bermuda is unpredictable and often windy. The rest of the year it is mild, much like the Carolinas. Some of my panelists found the Elderhostel program director too young and not too understanding.

Getting In: According to the Elderhostel catalog, all international programs receive more registration requests than there are spaces to be filled. I would expect early reservations are required for Bermuda, particularly during the height of the tourist season.

Getting There: Bermuda is only a short flight from most of our East Coast cities. A cruise ship, steamer, or freighter would be a pleasant alternative means of travel.

Brazil

Rio de Janeiro (week 1 of 3-week program)—University of Fluminense (Universidade Federal Fluminense)

Courses of Study: Rio's Art, Culture, and Society

Quality of Instructors: This program takes Elderhostelers to three different cities and three different academic institutions; therefore, it is not suprising to find varying degrees of skill and ability among the professors and lecturers.

Environment: Brazil encompasses almost one-half of the South American continent. The vegetation is tropical, subtropical, and equatorial, and the architecture a highly decorative baroque mix imported from Portugal and Spain. The churches are lavishly decorated with gold, diamonds, emeralds, and elaborate wood carvings. Rio de Janeiro may well be the most written-about city in the world. It is frequently described as a wild carnival, a city stretched along the beach that throbs with the sensual, African-inspired beat of the samba. The urban elite seem totally unaware of the misery of the favelas, the shacks that litter the mountainsides just outside of town.

Housing: Elderhostelers stay in modest hotels that have twin-bed rooms and private bathroom facilities. The hotel for the Rio week is air-conditioned and is located in Niteroi, a city just across the bridge. The location is lovely, right on the bay commanding, a gorgeous view of Rio both day and night.

Food: The meals served are excellent in all three cities. Brazilian food is a gastronomical experience, the national dish, feijoada, is a thick black bean stew garnished with manioc, an edible root, and pigs' ears and tails. Brazilian beer, called "chopp," is renowned and cachaça, the knock-your-socks-off traditional alcoholic beverage, is guaranteed to clear the sinuses.

Unique Attributes: Brazil is a country of vast ethnic and regional diversity, and Elderhostelers from North America have an opportunity to meet native Brazilians in three very different locations. All the field trips are stimulating and well designed, and a wealth of extra activities are offered as part of the Brazilian experience. Rio is a very cosmopolitan city of 10 million. Elderhostelers enjoy concerts and entertainment from around the world. During the summer of 1988, a traveling troupe of young Russian singers and dancers were performing in Rio during the Elderhostelers' stay.

Copacabana Beach is the focal point of life in Rio. It is a stage, where babies dig in the sand while joggers, surfers, and swimmers dodge the ever-present soccer and volleyball games. Businessmen in shirts and ties conduct business on the beach, while lines of barefooted samba dancers snake through the not-very-clean sand.

Shortcomings: Rio is dangerous, and crime is a huge problem, but the location of Niteroi some distance from the big city tends to lessen the stressful elements for the Elderhostel group. Tourists must learn not to wear or carry valuables.

Getting In: Be smart and book early—and do not forget to list alternate dates and destinations.

Getting There: The Brazilian program includes round-trip flight arrangements from Miami, Los Angeles, or New York City. The Elderhostel participants must pay all additional costs of add-on airfare from gateway cities in the states and any extended touring in the host country.

São Paulo (week 2 of 3)—University of São Paulo (Pontificia Universidade Catolica de São Paulo)

Courses of Study: Economy and Industry in São Paulo

Quality of Instructors: Most of the instructors received a grade of very good.

Environment: São Paulo is a city of some 15 million people. It is one of the most beautiful metropolises in the world. It boasts superb museums, skyscrapers, cathedrals and exotic restaurants. The urban elite, like their compatriots in Rio, are oblivious to the misery of the favelas, the slums of the malnourished indigents that hug the mountainsides just outside of town.

At the University of São Paulo, the largest of Brazil's twelve Catholic universities, Elderhostelers learn about the delicate educational and political problems facing the current democratic government.

Housing: The air-conditioned São Paulo hotel is fine but it is "not in a neighborhood comfortable for walking at night."

Unique Attributes: São Paulo is a cosmopolitan melting pot resembling New York City in many ways: the towering skyscrapers that light up at night are reminiscent of Manhattan, as is the first-class array of museums, zoo, art exhibits, and international restaurants. São Paulo's climate is cooler and windier than the climate in Rio. Remember: the seasons below the equator are the reverse of seasons in North America.

Shortcomings: "The automobile traffic in São Paulo is unbelievable," wrote a pair of New York City residents. "Travel to the university was time-consuming and hectic." They said it was almost worse than trying to fight your way crosstown in New York City at rush hour.

Getting There: Brazil is huge. It is the fifth-largest nation in the world and has an excellent internal air system. Travel between Rio and São Paulo is fast and frequent. Shuttle planes leave every half hour.

Ouro Preto (week 3 of 3)—Institute of Arts and Culture of the University of Ouro Preto (Universidade Federal de Ouro Preto)

Courses of Study: Ouro Preto, Jewel of Baroque Civilization and Cradle of the Brazilian Republic

Quality of Instructors: A few of the instructors in Brazil are not fluent in English, and a few are not very comfortable relating to the group of senior American participants.

Environment: Ouro Preto is an inland mining city in Minas Gerais. It is a gem of the colonial period restored to its elaborate elegance since its designation as a National Patrimony in 1933. The beauty of the city is breathtaking. It is scattered over a series of steep hills with wonderful views of the rich valleys below.

Housing: The accommodations in Ouro Preto are very good, except for the steep, winding cobblestone hills that must be climbed. The mountainous location of the hotel makes air-conditioning unnecessary.

Unique Attributes: Ouro Preto is one of this vast country's most picturesque areas. True to its name (meaning Black Gold), it is the mining center for gold and many semiprecious stones. Touring Ouro Preto offers one an opportunity to admire the rich cultural heritage of the country exhibited in eleven Baroque churches, the work of a famous, deformed, and crippled sculptor, Aleijadinho. Born in Ouro Preto he became Brazil's greatest artist.

Ouro Preto, Brazil. (Photo by Barbara L. Silvers)

Shortcomings: "Breathtaking" seems to be an appropriate word. My panelists found the steep hills "breath-shortening as well as breathtaking."

Getting There: The group flies from São Paulo to Belo Horizonte, the nearest inland city with an airport. They then board buses for a spectacular two-and-a-half-hour bus trip from Belo Horizonte to Ouro Preto over a newly paved road.

Canada

Lake Simcoe, Kempenfelt Centre— Georgian College

Courses of Study: Les multiples facettes du folklore canadien; Bien manger pour se sentir mieux; Les francophones de l'Ontario. This program is presented entirely in French for bilingual Elderhostelers only.

Quality of Instructors: Two of the three instructors were very good, but the third teacher spoke unintelligible Canadian French rather than Parisian French.

Environment: The Kempenfelt Centre is an attractive convention center stretched along the south shore of Lake Simcoe. Nearby are two popular Canadian resorts, Barrie and Orillia. Although Ontario was originally settled by the French, now only 10 percent of the population is French. Elderhostelers were invited to swim in the lake, but the summer weather was uncooperative.

Noisy, giant-size Canada geese honk and circle the lake with great frequency.

Housing: This program can accommodate a very large number of Elderhostelers in various residential facilities. When my reviewer was there, the school hosted two groups, one bilingual and one English-speaking.

The main building is quite modern, but my reviewer was housed in a two-story walk-up lodge that was pleasant and comfortable. Bathroom facilities are shared, but single rooms are available upon request.

Food: "Unbelievable," gushed my reviewer. "Real French chefs prepare superb desserts." The Elderhostel program filled the dining room for meals served in semi-cafeteria style. Some waitress assistance is provided.

Unique Attributes: My reviewer rated this program her favorite of the six she attended. "Very impressed— I'd go back again," she said. The physical plant is very comfortable with central lounges for socializing and good classrooms. Very worthwhile side trips are planned. The president of Georgian College establishes the cordial, informal atmosphere by welcoming the Elderhostelers at the orientation session.

My reviewer liked the center's proximity to Toronto. One can follow the Elderhostel program with a pleasant week of sight-seeing in that clean, shiny city of well-designed skyscrapers. The city can be toured comfortably on its good subway, bus, or streetcar systems. Toronto has excellent museums, galleries, and dinner theater.

Shortcomings: None reported.

Getting In: No problems noted by my reporter.

Getting There: All major Canadian airlines fly in and out of the Toronto International Airport. Elderhostelers taxi from the airport to the Centre. This program does not require the use of a private automobile.

Sudbury, Ontario—Cambrian College

Courses of Study: Fur Harvest of Ontario; Nickel; Images of a Mining Industry; Rocks, Rocks, Rocks (Geology)

Quality of Instructors: The teachers are an excellent group of serious-minded specialists.

Environment: Ontario was settled in the eighteenth century by the British and Scottish, while Quebec was settled by the French. Examples of this English heritage are visible throughout the province. North of Sudbury are cold, wild lakes, forests, and logging camps, while to the south one finds the industrial and agricultural areas of Ontario.

Sudbury is the nickel capital of the world and is located 250 miles north of the bustling city of Toronto, the commercial powerhouse of Canada. The Cambrian College campus is conveniently close to a world-class science center, and students are encouraged to make use of the facility.

Housing: The dormitories of the Regent Street Campus of Cambrian College only have single rooms with communal washrooms. My reviewers rated them "good."

Food: Meals for the Elderhostelers are served in the hospital cafeteria. "Not five star but good enough."

Unique Attributes: My reviewers found this program "one of the most fascinating, unusual and interesting

Elderhostels attended." A local transit bus stops right in front of the residence hall if one wishes to try the shopping and restaurants of Sudbury, and the field trips are well planned and well executed. Field trips to the nickel cauldrons in Sudbury offer students an opportunity to watch the hot slag spew forth like erupting volcanoes. During the heyday of the forties, Sudbury's mines poured out 92 percent of the Free World's nickel. Mines of zinc, silver, and copper are found in nearby Kidd Creek, and Elliot Lake is a rich source of uranium. This week is designed for hostelers interested in metals and minerals. This program offers a special opportunity for Elderhostelers to explore in depth the interdependency of the Canadian and American economies and be sensitized to the problems created by nuclear power and acid rain.

Shortcomings: "None worth noting," my reviewer wrote.

Getting In: No difficulties were encountered by my panelists.

Getting There: Air Canada jetliners have frequent service to Sudbury. In addition, the Canadian Pacific Railroad has Pullman service and daily trains from Montreal or Toronto. Sudbury sits on a crossroad of the Trans-Canada Highway.

China

Shijiazhuang (week 1 of 3-week program)—Hebei Teachers University

Courses of Study: History; Arts; Literature; Ancient and Modern China

Quality of Instructors: Very superior. The teaching profession is highly respected in China.

Environment: Shijiazhuang, the capital of Hebei Province, is a city not yet spoiled by tourism. My reviewer of the China program was a member of the very first Elderhostel group to walk through the "Open Door." Her daily journal is fascinating but too detailed for inclusion here. At the conclusion of the three weeks, she wrote, "I'll return glowing in reminiscences of the wonderful, hospitable people; of the overwhelming sense of history; of the fantastic national monuments; the palaces; the ancient flat-brick houses and—side by side—massive new apartment buildings and hotels going up so fast it's scary; the campaigns to curb family size, use refrigerators, stop spitting, combat noise pollution, and plant trees. With no campaign at all, the Chinese are kind to kids and grandparents."

Housing: "The best they have. Don't expect it to meet U.S. standards." Although my reviewer's group was

Elderhosteler returns to China to teach English, Shijiazhuang Railroad Station.

scheduled to be accommodated at the Hebei Guest House in double-occupancy rooms with private baths, they were displaced by a trade fair and had to stay in a second- or third-class hotel. "Despite the brand-new red carpet (the color red symbolizes good luck) laid in our honor, the bathrooms were barely adequate, bedrooms so-so and the food not up to the standard we had met elsewhere," she wrote.

Food: "Chop Suey fans stay home. You'll eat noodles and noodles and noodles. Have to request rice." The Chinese diet can pose problems for the uninitiated because of the heavy use of salt and cooking oil.

Unique Attributes: Before taking the three-hour train ride to Shijiazhuang, the group stays overnight in Beijing and visits the Forbidden City. The train itself is an experience, an excellent, air-conditioned coach espe-

First Elderhostel group in China, 1986.

cially reserved for the Elderhostel group. Trains are the major means of transportation in China, and the coaches are unbelievably crowded.

Excerpts from my reviewer's journal: "We hadn't known the full meaning of hospitality until we arrived in China. That evening we were honored guests of the Hebei provincial government at an extremely elaborate banquet. TV camera crews and ceremonial tea service and more red carpets. . . round tables hosted by members of the Hebei Provincial Education Commission. They sang to us. . . a goodly number of toasts were drunk that evening."

Getting In: The Elderhostel program in China seems able to accommodate a rather large group. Two buses were used to transport the group on the experience reviewed here.

Getting There: Elderhostelers embarking from the West Coast fly on JAL to Tokyo, stay overnight there, and then fly to Beijing and take the train to Shijiazhuang.

Beijing (week 2 of 3)—Hebei Medical College

Courses of Study: Chinese Medicine and Education

Quality of Instructors: All Elderhostel lecturers in China are superior.

Environment: China is still an exotic place to visit. It is not yet spoiled by tourism.

Housing: Even though Elderhostelers are treated to the best accommodations in China, on the whole these do not meet U.S. standards of comfort and sanitation. Bed pillows, for instance, are filled with millet rather than the feathers and foam we are accustomed to.

Food: The quality of the meals served varies greatly from place to place. Many lavish afternoon banquets are included in the program. Peking Duck is served so often it loses its reputation as a gourmet treat.

Unique Attributes: The Chinese Elderhostel staff are a group of eight to ten people who roll out the red carpet for their guests. "From the moment we were welcomed by provincial officers to the closing festive banquet, we were treated like visiting royalty in a most gracious manner. We were laden with gifts, relieved of our luggage by luggage handlers, and introduced to a staff that included a bookkeeper and general manager."

Elderhosteler in front of classroom at Hebei Medical College, Hebei Province, People's Republic of China.

"An Elderhostel in China is an unforgettable experience. I'm at a loss for words," wrote my reviewer, who later found the words and put them in a series of short stories. The classwork sensitizes Elderhostelers to the major problems of a country that has found itself catapulted into the twentieth century without passing through the social and industrial revolutions that Europe and the United States experienced during the eighteenth and nineteenth centuries.

Visits to a general hospital and demonstrations of acupuncture, manual massage, cupping, and moxibustion are followed by lectures on Chinese herbal medicine. "A bus trip to a nunnery passes through the heavily populated countryside over narrow roads teeming with bicyclists, donkey drawn carts, heavy transport trucks and hand-operated bikes for the lame, the sick and the halt . . . the city streets teem with pedestrians. We were intrigued by the sight of the street-sweeping persons."

Shortcomings: Be prepared to suffer some respiratory and/or gastrointestinal illness. Most Western travelers are not immune to the uniquely Chinese breed of germs. However, good medical service is available if needed, and your hosts are helpful about making the necessary arrangements.

Getting In: Early registration is essential.

Getting There: All internal travel is made by rail and bus. The native hosts make all of the arrangements.

Chengde (week 3 of 3)—Chengde Teachers College

Courses of Study: Daily evening lessons in the Chinese language and prebreakfast classes in t'ai chi (the graceful, ancient Chinese method of exercise) are offered as optional opportunities throughout the program. In Chengde excellent daily lectures continue on Ancient Chinese History, Urban and Rural Life, and Manners and Customs.

Quality of Instructors: Courteous, concerned, caring and intelligent.

Environment: This is a far cry from a Hilton/Hong Kong "shop till you drop" excursion in China. Chengde is located in beautiful mountainous country in the north.

Housing: "The best quarters of all," said my reviewer. It is a five-storied walk-up guest house, but Elderhostelers are assigned to first- and second-story rooms. Small two-bed rooms, each with a clean private bath. "Frugal but comfortable." Dormitory has a pleasant reading room on the ground floor.

Food: "And then there is tea, tea, tea!" Box lunch is provided on the train, and the dining room adjacent to the dormitory is very clean with quite elegant food service, "vases of silk flowers," and so forth. At the closing banquet, Elderhostelers painted a banner for the requisite gift exchange that said, "Happiness is being with our Chinese friends—Elderhostel, September

1986." "The dishes prepared for this farewell banquet are works of art—butterflies, mountains, a peacock."

Unique Attributes: "Greeted on our arrival in Chengde with a brass band and strings of exploding fireworks. . . students clapping and Elderhostelers moved to tears by the warmth of the welcome." Chengde is famous for its Buddhist and Tibetan temples. Elderhostelers are treated to concerts of the Chengde Folk Orchestra and Anhui Opera.

More excerpts from my reviewer's journal: "An evening reminiscent of long-ago soirées at the University of Chicago. . . invited by a group of retired and active scholars. . . sharing delicate little porcelain cups of wine, tea, grapes, cakes, and snowflake pears in a cheerful bed-sitting room in a faculty apartment. . . a gentle exchange of views with the help of an interpreter. . . hosts eager to learn our customs and ways."

Shortcomings: Do not expect Western standards of sanitation and plumbing in China. This is a country catapulted into the twentieth century without passing through some intermediary stages of development. The Elderhostel catalog emphatically and wisely cautions prospective travelers in frail health not to enroll in this program. My reviewer was extremely fatigued by the schedule, but this did not prevent her from returning to China the following year to spend six months teaching English, an invitation received while attending the Elderhostel.

Getting There: The train en route to Chengde passes right through a gap in the Great Wall. "We looked up and there it was!"

England

Durham—University of Durham/ Collingwood College

Courses of Study: Exploring the Prehistoric North; Gardens in England

Quality of Instructors: Lectures are given in the library, a nice, scholarly atmosphere conducive to learning.

Environment: This region of northeastern England touches the Scottish border and is opposite southern Scandinavia. The counties of Durham and Northumberland form the core of the ancient Kingdom of Northumbria—its history is more dramatic and turbulent than any other region of England.

The city of Durham exhibits all of the various influences and marks left by the successive periods of English history. There are scars left by battles of Pagans and Christians, roads built by Roman legions, wounds from the plunder of Vikings and Danes, and cathedrals and castles built by Norman barons.

Housing: Collingwood Hall of Residence is just ten minutes from the center of town and has beautiful views of the neighboring countryside.

Food: Typical English cuisine is served—roast beef with Yorkshire pudding.

Unique Attributes: To walk on Hadrian's Wall is the highlight of the three-week Elderhostel for some English history scholars. Visiting the roots of Great Britain's history and heritage can promote a greater understanding of the myriad forces that shaped the country's growth. The craggy coastline of Durham has been immortalized in the King Arthur legends, in which knights jousted on horseback and feasted at the Round Table.

Shortcomings: Bring along a trenchcoat—northeastern England can be cold and wet.

Getting In: My reviewers had no complaints.

Getting There: Durham is usually a one-week destination of a three-week Great Britain University Programme Schedule. Flights originating in the United States may land in London's Gatwick or Heathrow airports, or at Manchester, Prestwick, Dublin, or Shannon.

England, Scotland, Wales

London (week 1 of 3-week program)— London School of Economics

Courses of Study: Roman London: A Look at the Relics of 400 Years of Roman Rule; The Age of Elegance: Eighteenth-Century English Art; Elizabethan London.

Quality of Instructors: All of the professors are learned scholars and stimulate the students' interest. One attendee suggested that a microphone would have improved her course, since the teacher's voice was sometimes inaudible and the hearing of some of her classmates was less than perfect.

Environment: Only crowd-lovers should visit London, a city of great ethnic diversity with a unique character and sense of tradition. Contemporary London earns its reputation from its pubs, double-deckers, bobbies, and the amusing hats on the palace guards. Rosebery Hall is ideally located for window shopping in Piccadilly, discovering the National Gallery or British Museum, strolling through Hyde Park, or photographing the changing of the guard at Buckingham Palace. Rosebery Hall offers easy access to the Underground or the buses. Wellington Hall, used for some London programs, is within walking distance of the Tate Gallery, Buckingham Palace, Westminster Abbey, as well as the Victoria Underground station, train station, and buses.

Housing: Elderhostelers in Rosebery Hall have single rooms with communal bathroom facilities. The building does not have a lift, and one reviewer complained, "Rosebery Hall in London was the least attractive accommodation of the six Elderhostels I've attended." Wellington Hall has been refurbished since its original use as a residence hall for theological students of King's College. It has three floors of rooms with no lifts.

Food: On the average it is good at all three locations, and local specialties are served. In London that means Yorkshire Pudding. Do not forget to try fish and chips wrapped in newspaper, and a relaxing midafternoon tea with crustless tea sandwiches.

Unique Attributes: The Saga guide who accompanies the group is very proficient. He handles luggage, arranges all side trips, purchases theater tickets, and runs interference when problems arise. London has a vibrant entertainment scene. The theaters near Leicester Square are easily reached on the Tube or in London taxis, with their witty, well-informed drivers. Curtain time is early in London, and you will sit in "the stalls," not in the orchestra. Window-shopping on Regent Street or Bond Street in London is a not-to-be-missed treat, and if time permits, take a guidebook and find the London of Sherlock Holmes, Charles Dickens, or Geoffrey Chaucer. If you choose to spend some time shopping in Harrods, the famous department store, you may rub elbows with the Queen of England, who is reputed to be Harrods' most illustrious client.

Shortcomings: "Almost too much crammed into three weeks." "This is a great trip for the vigorous traveler." One couple, unhappy with Rosebery Hall, complained that the bathrooms are inconveniently located.

Getting In: Be smart—book early!

Getting There: The cost of the three-week package includes round-trip, regularly scheduled jet flight from gateway cities in the United States to London/ Heathrow Airport.

Glasgow (week 2 of 3-week England- Scotland-Wales program)—University of Strathclyde

Courses of Study: Scottish Heritage: Clans and Tartans; Scottish Heritage: Food, Drink, Culture

Quality of Instructors: An outstanding professor who knows how to liven the learning. "He illustrated his lectures with exhibits of native costumes and samples of food."

Environment: The bustling industrial city of Glasgow, Scotland's largest city, is at the heart of the region of Strathclyde. It is not nearly as romantic as the Scotland of Sir Walter Scott's novels, but one is apt to see sheep grazing on the hillsides. In Edinburgh, cobbled streets lead to the top of Castle Rock, where the great fortress of Edinburgh commands a view of the surrounding region just as it did in medieval times.

Housing: Murray Hall is a beautiful, modern building located on the grounds of the university in the heart of Glasgow. There is no lift, but the accommodations are rated very pleasant and comfortable, "almost fit for a king."

Food: Porridge for breakfast, cock-a-leekie soup, haggis, and Scottish flummery for dessert.

Unique Attributes: The highlight of the week seems to be a day spent in Edinburgh which includes a visit to the castle and an opportunity to enjoy theater within that mighty fortress. The day finishes with an entertaining display of dancers in traditional dress accompanied by the skirl of bagpipers. The Scots are very friendly people, and travelers find them always ready to engage in conversation. Some Elderhostelers have been lucky enough to be in Edinburgh during the annual festival, when the city throbs with music, dance, drama, and the wail of more bagpipers.

Shortcomings: One theater buff, accustomed to the New York City stage, reported, "Only two of seven cast members at the theater were half-decent actors."

Getting In: It is worth repeating. Be smart, book early!

Getting There: All internal flights and overnight stays in modest hotels near the airport, when required, are arranged by Saga Holidays, Ltd., and included in the cost of the tour package.

Bangor (week 3 of 3-week England-Scotland-Wales program)—University College of North Wales

Courses of Study: Welsh Music and Song: Welsh Heritage

Quality of Instructors: The teaching is splendid.

Environment: Wales is famed for its bleak landscape, singing people, and unpronounceable names. Bangor is in the heart of the most scenic area of Wales, where relics of the Celtic civilization and Roman occupation can be found. The Roman, Anglo-Saxon, and Norman influences can still be seen in Roman gold mines, Arthurian legends, and Norman castles.

Housing: Elderhostelers stay in single rooms in Plas Gwyn, a modern dormitory that does not have a lift for access to the upper floors.

Unique Attributes: The resident program coordinator in Wales is very efficient. The romantic myth of Camelot as well as the Celtic legends still live in Wales. There are not too many coal miners still singing on their homeward march from the collieries, but sheep roam freely in the meadows and the poetry of Dylan Thomas is recited in the classroom. The Welsh language is lovely and lyrical but very difficult for foreigners to master. This is not a problem, since most everyone speaks English.

Shortcomings: None reported.

Getting In: Moderately difficult.

Getting There: Travel arrangements are made to ensure that hostelers arrive at their first program as refreshed as can be reasonably expected. The outgoing flight is overnight (you arrive at your destination in the morning), while the homebound flight has travelers returning to the United States on the same day.

France

Chevreuse—Chateau De Meridon

Courses of Study: French Educational System; Social Policy; Architecture; Parks; Painting; Sculpture; Literature

Quality of Instructors: Very good. Visiting lecturers excellent.

Environment: Very pleasant. Located in a large country house surrounded by acres of grassy park built 100 years ago to replicate an eighteenth-century castle with tower and winding staircase. It was the home of a Portuguese banker, not the residence of a feudal lord or French nobleman. Only twenty miles from Paris, Chevreuse is a small village that invites one to stroll through the early morning open-air markets, their stalls piled high with fresh produce, wild mushrooms, and exotic cheeses.

Housing: Varies from decent to excellent. Some rooms share baths on the same floor while others enjoy private baths. Sleeping rooms are on the second and third floors of the chateau and also in a renovated farmhouse and barn about 250 yards from the main chateau. All rooms are double, and hostelers make their own beds in the tradition of the Dutch Folk School.

Food: Ambrosia. All meals are cooked by a resident French chef, and program participants assist in clearing tables after meals.

Unique Attributes: The director possesses an extensive knowledge of modern and classic architecture, painting, sculpture, and literature, as well as a special ability to share that knowledge. Much of the lecturing takes place on the bus as the group travels to field-trip sites. Time is very well organized in this program. Included are many thorough visits to Paris, off-the-beaten-path locations as well as the better-known attractions. Lectures are varied with excursions to places of general interest and informal discussions with natives in their homes, farms, and factories. Reviewers enjoyed staying in one location for three weeks of intensive living and learning. This program is designed and conducted by Scandinavian Seminars, Inc.

Shortcomings: My reviewer wrote, "No shortcomings. I spent every Saturday in Paris on my own." But some of the travelers in her group believed that the one hour's distance from Paris was a problem, although it was possible to taxi to and from the Metro station in St. Remy and get to Paris independently if one wished. There is little or no evening entertainment scheduled at the chateau—a weakness for some, while others found the days so full nothing further was needed.

Getting In: All European destinations are very popular and France one of the most desired. This chateau program is my reviewer's "number one pick of the lot" of ten Elderhostels, both domestic and foreign.

Getting There: Fly to and from Paris from your gateway city in the United States with an airfare that permits a stay of up to 180 days.

Israel

Tel Aviv (week 1 of 3-week program)— Beit Berl University

Courses of Study: Israel, Holy Land to Three Major Faiths; Jews and Arabs in Israel; Israel—A Pluralistic Society

Quality of Instructors: The professors are all excellent, effective teachers.

Environment: Israel is a country of some 4 million people jammed into a space the size of Maryland. It is a land where the conflict between faith and reason still rages and the conflict of orthodoxy vs. nationalism continues. Beit Berl's campus is reminiscent of a rural Israeli settlement. The pastoral setting encourages students to spend much time outdoors enjoying the green lawns, tropical flowers, and palm-tree-lined paths.

Housing: On-campus housing is offered in a one-story dormitory building that contains double rooms, each with a private bathroom and shower.

Food: The food served in the cafeteria is good and plentiful. Jewish dietary laws are observed; milk and meat are not served at the same meal, which may or may not

Roman aqueduct, Caesarea, Israel. (Photo by Ellen M. Reardon)

be noticeable until the cream substitute is offered with one's coffee. Tel Aviv is peopled primarily by descendants of Eastern European immigrants, and the cuisine reflects this influence. Israel is a melting pot, so other dietary influences can be found. These include recipes devised by Spanish Sephardic Jews, Arabs, French, and North Africans.

Unique Attributes: "Extraordinarily well-versed guides" lead the Elderhostelers on a broad variety of field trips and activities to illustrate the subjects being studied in the classroom. Synagogues, mosques, churches, and educational institutions are visited, as well as a Jewish kibbutz and an Arab settlement where discussions are held with Arab students.

Tel Aviv is a glittering city, home to the Israel Philharmonic and an active theater. Sidewalk cafes line broad boulevards in front of five-star hotels. Elderhostelers are treated to an evening at the theater in Tel Aviv. They are the only members of the audience supplied with earphones through which the Hebrew dialogue is instantaneously translated into English.

Shortcomings: Absolutely no shortcomings were noted.

Getting In: In case the Israel program you request is filled without resorting to a registration lottery, I would urge early booking. A very enthusiastic husband and wife wrote as follows: "This was our first Elderhostel. All else is commentary."

Getting There: El Al Airlines is used for nonstop jet service from New York to Tel Aviv. Special add-on fares to New York from other United States cities are available, and the fare permits up to a two-month stay in Israel.

Jerusalem (week 2 of 3)—Hebrew University

Courses of Study: Jerusalem in the Light of Archaeology; The Bible and the Land; Jerusalem, Past and Present

Quality of Instructors: The professors are superb in this institution, Israel's first school of higher learning.

Western Wall, Jerusalem, Israel. (Photo by Ellen M. Reardon)

Environment: The university is located in the city of Jerusalem, the eternal city sacred to the three religions of Christianity, Islam, and Judaism. A city of contrast: one can go from the Arab quarters, where minarets pierce the sky above the mosques, to the ultra-Orthodox district, where men wear beards and long side-curls and the women are all modestly dressed. Jerusalem is a modern city of almost one-half million inhabitants that has been continuously inhabited for 5,000 years—a rather mind-boggling concept.

Housing: Among my panel of reviewers are Elder-hostelers who stayed in both the Zohar Hotel and the Beit Maiersdorf Faculty Club. The Zohar is a new hotel in a lovely neighborhood of Jerusalem overlooking the

Judean Desert. It is fully air-conditioned and heated and has elevator service, and in addition, all rooms have private baths, telephones, and radios. The Faculty Club is located on the university's Mount Scopus campus. All guest rooms have the same niceties as the Zohar Hotel. Both the hotel and the Faculty Club received hosannas.

Food: One couple from the East Coast of the United States wrote, "Great food if you like chicken!" The influence of immigrants from the Middle East predominates in Jerusalem. Chick-peas ground into "hummus bi tahini" is a favorite appetizer.

Unique Attributes: "If you've never seen the Judean desert by moonlight, you still have a thrill in store for you." Elderhostelers who have been to Jerusalem before observed, "Now that safety has become a factor in big cities, we find a major advantage in Elderhosteling is traveling in a group of such high-caliber people." In years past, this couple traveled extensively throughout the Middle East alone.

By studying the sources and manifestations of the Arab-Israeli conflict firsthand, one gains a deeper understanding of how difficult it is to maintain civility and values in a country under siege. The program week in Jerusalem usually includes an opportunity to float in the Dead Sea and a visit to the Ein Gedi Nature Reserve, where one can observe ibex leaping among the rocks and watch desert streams rush down the mountainside.

Shortcomings: One pair of panelists would have preferred housing closer to the center of the city, even though both facilities had easy and frequent public bus service into the city.

Getting There: From the beaches of Tel Aviv it is a forty-five-minute drive along a four-lane thruway to Jerusalem.

Haifa (week 3 of 3)—University of Haifa

Courses of Study: Media and the Image of Israel; Political Processes in Israel

Quality of Instructors: The faculty is superb.

Environment: The University of Haifa perches atop the crest of Mt. Carmel with a breathtaking view of the coastline, Mt. Hermon, and the Galilee. Haifa is the third largest city in Israel situated only forty kilometers from the Lebanese border. The country's largest concentration of heavy industry lies to the east of the city, and heavy maritime traffic passes through its port. The sense of danger and perpetual conflict on the borders dominates this area. The reasons Israel is burdened with astronomical defense costs are all too visible here.

Housing: Elderhostelers stay at the Kibbutz Beit Oren, an agricultural kibbutz four miles from the university. Each double room has its own bathroom, and the guest houses have lounges, social halls, and a swimming pool.

Food: Homegrown fresh fruits and dairy products are served, along with wonderful oranges, dates, persimmons, and wine pressed from their own vineyards.

Unique Attributes: Many of the early tenets of the kibbutzim have been altered, but the self-sufficient, communal agricultural society is still a unique Israeli phenomenon. Men and women still plow the fields side by side, and some children are raised communally. But drip irrigation has revolutionized Israeli agriculture, and the family takes a greater role in child-rearing than in the past. Kibbutz members still share property and eat in a communal dining hall.

Southeast of Haifa, the ancient people, the Druzes, live in small villages, and a visit to a Druze village is one of the Elderhostel field trips. Evenings at the Haifa Symphony and the Israeli Dance Theater are also arranged.

Shortcomings: None reported.

Getting In: According to the national registration department, all overseas program are much in demand.

Getting There: See information on week number one of the Israel program.

Italy

Sorrento—Trinity College, Hartford, Massachusetts

Courses of Study: Volcanology; Neapolitan Music; Art and Architecture

Environment: Sorrento is a gorgeous resort city that overlooks the clear, crystal-blue water of the Bay of Naples. Tourists have long flocked to Sorrento and the nearby island of Capri for their physical beauty, significant history, and enchantment, all of which have been recorded in song. It is said that a visit to Sorrento is guaranteed to reawaken the sentimental memories of aging romantics.

Housing: Elderhostelers enjoy living in an excellent luxury hotel. The rooms (doubles with private baths) have accommodated an impressive list of illustrious guests: Milton, Goethe, Byron, Shelly, Scott, and Ibsen, to name a few.

The hotel and its beautiful gardens are a short stroll from the city center.

Food: "Fabulous."

Unique Attributes: The splendid field trips take Elderhostelers to Mt. Vesuvius, the Naples Opera House, Pompeii, the Sorrento Cathedral and Museum, as well as Positano and the Greek settlement of Cuma. Cuma is the site of the Grotto of the Sibyl, immortalized by Virgil in the *Aeneid*. The Archaeological Museum in Naples is reputed to be the most interesting archaeological museum in the world. Frescoes, silverware, and artifacts prove the elegance of life in Pompeii before A.D. 79. This program highlights many of the glories of Italy.

"To spend two weeks in the charming fishing village of Sorrento, with its snow-white stone houses scattered along the cliffs, is a lifelong dream come true." Unpacking once for a two-week sojourn is one of the enticements of this program.

"If you are brave, and have time to stay after the Elderhostel, rent a car and see Amalfi and the fabled Amalfi Drive!" This curving road twists precipitously along the crest of the rocky headland, where every turn of the road opens up a vista more beautiful than the last. "Just go!"

Shortcomings: "The Elderhostel leader was an excellent teacher but an uncaring person. Couldn't be bothered with people."

Getting In: No difficulties were experienced by our panelists.

Getting There: New York is the gateway city for all Italian destinations. The airfare used for these programs entitles travelers to stay on for a maximum of twenty-one days.

Mexico

Oaxaca—Southern Illinois University at Carbondale

Courses of Study: Spanish Language and Hispanic Culture (a two-week program)

Quality of Instructors: The Southern Illinois teachers are competent, not inspiring.

Environment: Oaxaca, the capital of the state of Oaxaca, is situated in the deep south portion of Mexico, 315 miles south of Mexico City. It is a center of high-quality native crafts, particularly weaving and embroidery done in bright primary colors on simple back-looms. The women dye, card, and spin their own wool. The city, with a current population of 100,000 people, was founded in 1522 by a group of Spanish soldiers. The laid-back atmosphere of the mostly Indian people is vastly different from bustling Mexico City. The predominant architecture is Spanish Colonial, with many buildings built of the local pale-green stone.

Housing: My reviewers found the accommodations in the small hotel adequate. The hotel is in the heart of the city of Oaxaca across the street from the central park. Each double-occupancy room has its own bath. Single rooms are available upon request.

Food: "Mundane," was the pithy comment of my panelist. Program tuition does not include the noon meal; only breakfast and dinner are served to participants.

Unique Attributes: Since the Spanish language is here to stay as a regional language, this course offers an excellent opportunity for one to practice language skills, see basic Mexican life, and absorb a smattering of Mexican history, arts, cinema, and culture. Nearby are unusual examples of pre-Columbian ruins and artifacts. The main feature of Oaxaca is the weekly market held each Saturday, where vendors dressed in striped serapes and brilliant-colored rebozos hawk their wares on the cobblestone streets. Straw-hatted men, hidden behind mounds of red and green chilies, sell hand-embroidered blouses and hangings. It is a city of bell-ringing churches and shady trees.

Shortcomings: The class is too large and accepts individuals with such a wide range of ability and experience that the language instruction becomes too slow for the more advanced members of the group. One panelist found two weeks in Oaxaca "too long."

Getting In: This is a much-sought-after destination. "Getting in is very difficult. I didn't make it until my third try," one reviewer complained.

Getting There: Individuals need to make their own travel arrangements to Oaxaca. Mexico's two national airlines, Aeromexico and Mexicana, have connecting daily flights through Guadalajara or Mexico City. One can also reach Oaxaca on an overnight train from Mexico City. The Pan-American Highway from Mexico City to Oaxaca is currently being improved by the Mexican government.

Danza del Sol on Lake Chapala— University of Oklahoma (in cooperation with the Universidad Autonoma de Guadalajara)

Courses of Study: Folk Art and Music of Mexico (a ten-day program)

Quality of Instructors: The teachers were inadequately informed about their subjects. "Give them a C," one reviewer wrote.

Environment: Located at a resort in the midst of spectacularly beautiful gardens between Lake Chapala and the mountains, thirty miles southeast of Guadalajara. The drive to the lake traverses one of Mexico's most scenic stretches, where one can observe farms still tilled by oxen and burros en route to market. The terraced gardens of the resort overlook a swimming pool and lighted tennis courts. Guadalajara, the second-largest city in Mexico, is not yet troubled with the smog of Mexico City, but it does have an exploding population. Lake Chapala is the largest lake in Mexico.

Housing: Elderhostelers reside in a beautiful resort-like facility with fancy furnishings and service. Danza del Sol is a colonial Mexican building with one- and two-bedroom suites that include a living room and private bath.

Food: Elegant meals and fresh papayas and mangoes are served outdoors in restaurant style. Try some fiery tequila, the national alcoholic beverage, or some delicious native dark beer.

Unique Attributes: The Danza del Sol is a beautiful posh facility, something not often found in Elderhosteling. The field trips to Guadalajara's museums, theaters, and market day are well organized and very interesting. The little lakeside villages with narrow cobblestone streets are filled with natives selling hand-loomed textiles and pottery. Nearby Ajijic is a thriving artist colony. The lake, edged with colorful water hyacinths, is used for boating, swimming, and fishing. Lake Chapala's whitefish can be found on menus throughout Mexico.

Shortcomings: None.

Getting In: I am afraid you will have to participate in a lottery for this one.

Getting There: Guadalajara is easily accessible by air. Many major carriers service this city. In the winter months Mexico thrives on tourism so one may have to make plane reservations before the Elderhostel lottery is completed.

Nova Scotia

Mahone Bay—Oak Island Inn

Courses of Study: Lunenburg, Our Heritage; Theatrical Product and Performance; The Mystery of Oak Island

Quality of Instructors: Local people and professionals from the Fisheries Museum of the Atlantic in Lunenburg. Very good and very interesting.

Environment: Nova Scotia (New Scotland) was founded by Scots escaping oppression and poverty in their homeland. Much of the country is bleak and foggy, a vista that encourages all the myths about pirates and hidden treasures. Little old towns and villages dot the South Shore facing the Atlantic. The shoreline of Nova Scotia is frequently shrouded by pea-soup fog. I vividly remember a week when my husband and I were imprisoned by fog in Sydney, Nova Scotia, waiting for a flight to the island of St. Pierre. We finally gave up and boarded an overnight ferry for the crossing.

The natives and local tradespeople are friendly and forthcoming, a proud rural people of very mixed heritage. The province was settled by French, Scottish, Irish, and New Englanders. Fishing and shipbuilding have always been a major force in the economy, and the native shipbuilders built fine schooners. The Inn is situated on the bay, only forty-five miles from Halifax. The climate of Nova Scotia is very pleasant. The influence of the sea makes it cooler in summer and warmer in winter than one would expect that far north. The fine scenery and fascinating history make the province a favorite tourist destination, particularly the coastal drive known as the Cabot Trail.

Housing: Elderhostelers stay in nice rooms in the Inn. The Inn also has a heated swimming pool, sauna, and jacuzzi.

Food: "Lousy, but only for the Elderhostelers. It is skimpy and not very good." A different menu is served to the regular hotel guests.

Unique Attributes: The Inn is located across a small body of water from famous Oak Island. Among the many Oak Island myths is one that Captain Kidd buried a stash there. My Elderhostel reviewers were not permitted on the island in May 1988, because the world-famous treasure hunt had been renewed. The Mahone Bay treasure hunt is a search that has lasted some 193 years, and has cost the lives of six men and millions of dollars. As part of the program, Elder-hostelers spend an interesting day on an inland farm that has been refurbished into its original state. However, no transportation was furnished. Hostelers with cars invited other attendees to join them.

Shortcomings: The Oak Tree Inn is a regular tourist hostelry. "The young lady in charge of the Elderhostel program has no idea what she should be doing. We were on our own for most activities. I would not go back to the Inn—might return to Nova Scotia." Skimpy meals as noted above are another complaint.

Getting In: If this program had waiting and standby lists in the past, I doubt that it will continue to have them.

Getting There: Taxi trip from Halifax airport is expensive—sixty dollars one way. The Scottish cabbie who drove my panelists on their return to the airport tried to make amends by taking them on a complimentary sight-seeing side trip.

Portugal

Braga—Centro Apostolico do Sameiro

Courses of Study: Influence of the Church in Braga

Quality of Instructors: Excellent.

Environment: The Centro is a small, private school affiliated with the Catholic Church. The modern buildings of the school command a spectacular view of Braga, the capital of the northern province of Minho. The influence of the church pervades the city. It is said that Braga's archbishops have been known to wield greater power than the king. The city attracts many pilgrimages to visit the shrine of Bom Jesus and is the home of Holy Week processions and colorful religious festivals, during which the villagers sing and dance through the streets.

Housing: Elderhostelers stay in very comfortable twin-bedded rooms with private bath facilities. Many rooms also have balconies.

Food: Delicious. Includes round loaves of country bread, hot out of the wood-burning oven, fresh seafood, and very sweet desserts.

Shepherd in Portugal. (Photo by Barbara L. Silvers)

Unique Attributes: The ambience of Portugal is colorful and lively, and this province of Minho is considered the most vivacious. The Romanesque jewels and adorned columns in the churches, the brilliant reds and blues of the regional costumes of the peasant women, and the paper flowers all contribute to the festival atmosphere. Trellises of grapes are everywhere, winding between gardens, edging the rooftops of the white cottages, and built against the almond and fig trees. Elderhostelers visit palaces, churches, and the lovely old town of Viana do Castelo at the mouth of River Lima on the Atlantic Ocean.

Shortcomings: None reported.

Getting In: The Spain/Portugal programs are much in demand.

Getting There: Overnight transatlantic flights from the United States arrive in either Spain or Portugal. Apex fares allow for a stay of 180 days. Cost of the flight and program varies according to the gateway city chosen.

Spain

Madrid, Granada, Córdoba, Segovia, and Barcelona—University of Madrid; University of Córdoba; University of Barcelona

Courses of Study: The Moorish Period in Spain; Cátalan Culture; Great Painters of the Twentieth Century; Granada—A Study of a Historic City

Quality of Instructors: Reviewers reported all instructors either excellent or outstanding.

Environment: A beautiful country full of magic moments and castles sitting on the highest hills. From the sight of Picasso's *Guernica* hanging in the Prado Museum in Madrid to the cave dwellings in Granada, this Saga-organized study adventure includes a heavy dose of history, monuments, and castles, and a light sampling of flamenco and tarantella. Madrid is a handsome city of palaces and plazas; Segovia, an ancient city; Barcelona, the mecca for Spanish artists; Maimonides is memorialized in Córdoba; and the tombs of Ferdinand and Isabella are in the Royal Chapel of Granada's cathedral.

The Alhambra, Granada, Spain. (Photo by Barbara L. Silvers)

Housing: The accommodations received both yeas and nays. "Mediocre to superb," one traveler reported, and "good in hotels but wonderful in homestays," wrote another hosteler. For her homestay in Segovia, one of my reviewers was assigned an Elderhostel roommate.

Food: "Usually very good but very different from the usual American diet." "Inconsistent," commented another hosteler. The colorful "tapa bars" that line the streets are a great way to sample local specialties, tasty sardine treats, or other nibbles in rich, yellow olive oil. Dinner hour in Spain is much later than is customary in the United States.

Unique Attributes: Too many to enumerate. All my reviewers were on two- or three-week programs and spent one week in each destination. The social homestay week in Segovia was the highlight of one Elderhosteler's journey to Spain. "Before you go," she wrote, "learn as much Spanish language as you can. It will enhance your experience immeasurably. Do not," she continued, "expect everyone in Spain to speak English!" She particularly enjoyed accompanying her hostess to market, to visit old churches, and to the public square.

Other highlights include guided tours to the fourteenth-century Alhambra in Granada, where you tour the great Moorish palace and its luxurious gardens with some 20,000 other visitors per day; a day as guests of the mayor in Santa Fe de Granada; the working Roman aqueduct in Segovia; or viewing collections of the work of Catalonian artists Pablo Picasso, Joan Miró, and Salvador Dali while in Barcelona. Whether driving through fields of sunflowers and earthy-smelling vineyards or viewing the dramatic

Spanish countryside and town. (Photo by Barbara L. Silvers)

vistas of the snow-capped Pyrenees, the countryside is rich with unexpected pleasures.

Shortcomings: The bus travel between cities is long and arduous, the roads narrow and curvy. All my evaluators complained about the length of the bus rides.

Getting In: "Vaya con Dios."

Getting There: Apex airfare for Spain and Portugal programs permits a stay of 180 days. All flights from gateway cities in the United States are routed through New York City for overnight flights to Madrid, Barcelona, or Lisbon.

Turkey

Istanbul (week 1 of a 3-week program)—The University of Istanbul in conjunction with Saga Holidays, Ltd.

Courses of Study: The Byzantine Civilization and the Ottoman Empire and Arts

Quality of Instructors: "Less than excellent."

Environment: Elderhostel classes are held in the heart of this city of intrigue, beauty, and mystery; a city that is now struggling with twentieth-century problems of bumper to bumper traffic, water shortages, crowding, and chaos.

Turkey is a large Middle Eastern country situated between the Black Sea and the Mediterranean. The first president of the Republic, Kemal Ataturk, replaced the fez, the veil, and the harem with industry in 1923. Ataturk modernized the political, social, and religious life of Turkey, but for Americans, Istanbul is still an exotic travel experience.

Housing: Hostelers are accommodated in the Klas Hotel, a good tourist-class establishment a short walk from the classrooms. The hotel has elevator service and provides a separate lounge for the Elderhostelers' use.

Food: "Excellent for our taste," wrote my panel members. The couple who submitted this review of the Turkey Elderhostel are not only veteran hostelers but have been journeying to this Middle Eastern republic since 1959. "We particularly love the sweet, thick Turkish coffee."

Unique Attributes: In Istanbul, Elderhostelers visit the 500-year-old indoor Bazaar and observe suppliants at prayer in the renowned Blue Mosque with its slender minarets, see the fabulous jewel collection in the Sultan's Topkapi Palace, and the splendid Byzantine mosaics in the Haghia Sophia Museum. "The color, sounds, and smells of the trip are memorable."

Shortcomings: Most of us have a smattering of Romance languages—French, German, Italian or Spanish remembered from high school or college —but the Turkish language is thoroughly unfamiliar. This adds a dimension of distance and exoticism to the excursion. "Some hostelers found the language barrier a problem. We couldn't decipher street signs, menus, or newspapers, but the friendliness and hospitality of our teachers, hosts, and the people compensated for this difficulty."

Getting In: The popularity of this program is well deserved.

Getting There: Elderhostelers depart from one of many gateway cities in the United States and fly to Istanbul for the first seven nights of the program. They return to Istanbul for the last night before departing for home.

Ankara and Aksaray in Cappodocia (week 2 of 3)—University of Ankara

Courses of Study: The Hittite and Phrygian Arts and the Valley of Cappodocia

Quality of Instructors: The Faculty of Turkish History and Arts are excellent. In Cappodocia lectures are held in an outdoor amphitheater.

Environment: Ankara, the capital city of Turkey, is a modern city of almost 2 million inhabitants. Gleaming skyscrapers and elegant residences vie with squatters' shacks that huddle on the fringe of the city. The streets throb with heavy traffic and pugnacious taxi drivers reminiscent of New York City, while in the pastoral plains to the east, shepherds tend their flocks of sheep. The region of Cappodocia holds a unique place in Turkish history, dating back to the arrival of the Hittites in 1700 B.C. Folklore explains the terrain as an invading army turned to stone, but modern geology describes the area as formed of volcanic rock.

Housing: In Ankara Elderhostelers stay in the Evkuran Hotel in twin-bed rooms with private baths. This nice tourist-class hotel is situated a short distance from the lecture rooms and has elevator service. In Aksary in the Cappodocia region, hostelers stay in the Agacli Motel. My reviewers found this motel excellent and raved about the lovely gardens.

Unique Attributes: In Ankara one becomes sensitive to Turkey's precarious location, geographically bridging Europe and Asia. In the Cappodocia region, until recently, peasants inhabited old cave dwellings that date back to 3000 B.C. Elderhostelers also visit a labyrinth of underground cities tunneled into the rock, where ancient tribes hid from invading armies. Once upon a time, camel caravans plodded through Cappodocia.

Getting In: Early registration required.

Getting There: From Istanbul the group boards an air-conditioned coach for the ride to Ankara. After five nights in Ankara, they reboard the bus for the trip to Aksaray, where they spend nights six and seven of week number two.

Ephesus (week 3 of 3)—Aegean University at Izmir

Courses of Study: The Civilization of Western Anatolia

Quality of Instructors: The professors, from the Archaeological Section of the Aegean University, are excellent.

Environment: Izmir (Seljuk) is a port on the Aegean Sea. The ancient archaeological sites of the area of Western Anatolia reveal the myriad influences of Turkey's history—influences of Persians, Greeks, Romans, Byzantines, Armenians, and Kurds. Although 99 percent of Turks practice the Muslim religion, the conflicting forces and ideologies of its ethnic history create a country that is an intriguing amalgamation of cultures. Ephesus, founded between 1500 and 1600 B.C., is now being reconstructed in its former splendor after being excavated by archaeologists. The multifaceted history of Ephesus includes Greek, Roman, and barbarian invaders, as well as destruction by Mongols and Christians in the Crusades.

Housing: The AK Hotel in Seljuk is very simple. It is a walk-up building, and the hike up to the third and fourth floors requires a healthy heart. The accommodations are in twin-bed rooms with private bath facilities. The hotel is in a village just three kilometers from Ephesus and is ideally located for visiting the other archaeological sites of the region.

Unique Attributes: Elderhostel classes are held in the old Seldjukie baths, now converted into a conference hall, belonging to the Ephesus Museum. The hotel, museum, and lecture rooms are all conveniently located near one another. A field trip to the ancient city of Troy on a fertile plain in Asia Minor brings to mind the legends of Homer's *Iliad* and *Odyssey*. In the sacred city of Ephesus, Elderhostelers visit the Temple of Diana, one of the seven wonders of the world.

Getting In: Early registration required.

Getting There: Elderhostelers arrive in Izmir on a Turkish Airlines flight from Ankara. The trip from Ephesus back to Istanbul is made in modern, air-conditioned coach buses. The flight back to the United States is on a regularly scheduled airline with brief stops en route.

OTHER BOOKS FROM JOHN MUIR PUBLICATIONS

22 Days Series: Travel Itinerary Planners
These pocket-size guides are a refreshing departure from ordinary guidebooks.
Each author has in-depth knowledge of the region covered and offers 22
carefully tested daily itineraries. Included are not only "must see" attractions
but also little-known villages and hidden "jewels" as well as valuable general
information. 128 to 144 pp., $7.95 each
22 Days in Alaska by Pamela Lanier (28-68-0)
22 Days in the American Southwest by Richard Harris (28-88-5)
22 Days in Asia by Roger Rapoport and Burl Willes (65-17-3)
22 Days in Australia by John Gottberg (65-03-3)
22 Days in California by Roger Rapoport (28-93-1)
22 Days in China by Gaylon Duke and Zenia Victor (28-72-9)
22 Days in Europe by Rick Steves (65-05-X)
22 Days in France by Rick Steves (65-07-6)
22 Days in Germany, Austria & Switzerland by Rick Steves (65-02-5)
22 Days in Great Britain by Rick Steves (28-67-2)
22 Days in Hawaii by Arnold Schuchter (28-92-3)
22 Days in India by Anurag Mathur (28-87-7)
22 Days in Japan by David Old (28-73-7)
22 Days in Mexico by Steve Rogers and Tina Rosa (65-04-1)
22 Days in New England by Anne E. Wright (28-96-6)
22 Days in New Zealand by Arnold Schuchter (28-86-9)
22 Days in Norway, Denmark & Sweden by Rick Steves (28-83-4)
22 Days in the Pacific Northwest by Richard Harris (28-97-4)
22 Days in Spain & Portugal by Rick Steves (65-06-8)
22 Days in the West Indies by Cyndy and Sam Morreale (28-74-5)

"Kidding Around" Travel Guides for Children
Written for kids eight years of age and older. Generously illustrated in two
colors with imaginative characters and images. Each guide is an adventure to
read and a treasure to keep.
Kidding Around San Francisco, Rosemary Zibart (65-23-8) 64 pp., $9.95
Kidding Around Washington, D.C., Anne Pedersen (65-25-4) 64 pp., $9.95
Kidding Around London, Sarah Lovett (65-24-6) 64 pp., $9.95

All-Suite Hotel Guide: The Definitive Directory, Pamela Lanier
Pamela Lanier, author of The Complete Guide to Bed & Breakfasts, Inns &
Guesthouses, now provides the discerning traveler with a listing of over 600
all-suite hotels. (65-08-4) 285 pp., $13.95

Asia Through the Back Door, Rick Steves and John Gottberg
Provides information and advice you won't find elsewhere—including how to
overcome culture shock, bargain in marketplaces, observe Buddhist temple
etiquette, and even how to eat noodles with chopsticks! (28-58-3) 336 pp.,
$11.95

Buddhist America: Centers, Practices, Retreats, Don Morreale
The only comprehensive directory of Buddhist centers, this guide includes
first-person narratives of individuals' retreat experiences. (28-94-X) 312 pp.,
$12.95

Bus Touring: Charter Vacations, U.S.A., Stuart Warren with Douglas Bloch
For many people, bus touring is the ideal, relaxed, and comfortable way to see
America. Covers every aspect of bus touring to help passengers get the most
pleasure for their money. (28-95-8) 200 pp., $9.95

Catholic America: Self-Renewal Centers and Retreats, Patricia Christian-Meyers
Complete directory of over 500 self-renewal centers and retreats in the United
States and Canada. (65-20-3) 325 pp., $13.95

**Complete Guide to Bed & Breakfasts, Inns & Guesthouses in the United States
and Canada,** 1989-90 Edition, Pamela Lanier
Newly revised and the most complete directory available, with over 5,000
listings in all 50 states, 10 Canadian provinces, Puerto Rico, and the U.S.
Virgin Islands. (65-09-2) 520 pp., $14.95

Elegant Small Hotels: A Connoisseur's Guide, Pamela Lanier
This lodging guide for discriminating travelers describes hotels characterized
by exquisite rooms and suites and personal service par excellence. (65-10-6)
230 pp., $14.95

Europe 101: History & Art for the Traveler, Rick Steves and Gene Openshaw
The first and only jaunty history and art book for travelers makes castles,
palaces, and museums come alive. (28-78-8) 372 pp., $12.95

Europe Through the Back Door, Rick Steves
For people who want to enjoy Europe more and spend less money doing it. In
this revised edition, Steves shares more of his well-respected insights.
(28-84-2) 404 pp., $12.95
Doubleday and Literary Guild Book Club Selection.

Gypsying After 40: A Guide to Adventure and Self-Discovery, Bob Harris
Retirees Bob and Megan Harris offer a witty and informative guide to the
"gypsying" life-style that has enriched their lives and can enrich yours. Their
message is: "Anyone can do it!" (28-71-0) 312 pp., $12.95

The Heart of Jerusalem, Arlynn Nellhaus
Arlynn Nellhaus draws on her vast experience in and knowledge of Jerusalem
to give travelers a rare inside view and practical guide to the Golden City.
(28-79-6) 312 pp., $12.95

Mona Winks: Self-Guided Tours of Europe's Top Museums, Rick Steves and
Gene Openshaw
Here's a guide that will save you time, shoe leather, and tired muscles. It is
designed for people who want to get the most out of visiting the great
museums of Europe. (28-85-0) 450 pp., $14.95

The On and Off the Road Cookbook, Carl Franz and Lorena Havens
A multitude of delicious alternatives to the usual campsite meals. (28-27-3)
272 pp., $8.50

The People's Guide to Mexico, Carl Franz
This classic guide shows the traveler how to handle just about any situation
that might arise while in Mexico.
"The best 360-degree coverage of traveling and short-term living in Mexico
that's going." — *Whole Earth Epilog* (28-99-0) 587 pp., $14.95

The People's Guide to RV Camping in Mexico, Carl Franz and Lorena Havens
This revised guide focuses on the special pleasures and challenges of RV travel
in Mexico. Includes a complete campground directory. (28-91-5) 304 pp., $13.95

The Shopper's Guide to Mexico, Steve Rogers and Tina Rosa
The only comprehensive handbook for shopping in Mexico, this guide ferrets
out little-known towns where the finest handicrafts are made and offers tips
on shopping techniques. (28-90-7) 200 pp., $9.95

Traveler's Guide to Asian Culture, Kevin Chambers
An accurate and enjoyable guide to the history and culture of this diverse
continent. (65-14-9) 356 pp., $13.95

Traveler's Guide to Healing Centers and Retreats in North America, Martine
Rudee and Jonathan Blease
Over 300 listings offer a wide range of healing centers—from traditional to
new age. (65-15-7) 224 pp., $11.95

Undiscovered Islands of the Caribbean, Burl Willes
For the past decade, Burl Willes has been tracking down remote Caribbean
getaways. Here he offers complete information on 32 islands. (28-80-X)
220 pp., $12.95

Automotive Repair Manuals
Each JMP automotive manual gives clear step-by-step instructions together
with illustrations that show exactly how each system in the vehicle comes
apart and goes back together. They tell everything a novice or experienced
mechanic needs to know to perform periodic maintenance, tune-ups,
troubleshooting, and repair of the brake, fuel and emission control, electrical,
cooling, clutch, transmission, driveline, steering and suspension systems and
even rebuild the engine.
How to Keep Your VW Alive (65-12-2) 410 pp., $17.95
How to Keep Your Golf/Jetta/Rabbit Alive (65-21-1) 420 pp., $17.95
How to Keep Your Honda Car Alive (28-55-9) 272 pp., $17.95
How to Keep Your Subaru Alive (65-11-4) 420 pp., $17.95
How to Keep Your Toyota Pick-Up Alive (28-89-3) 400 pp., $17.95
How to Keep Your Datsun/Nissan Alive (28-65-6) 544 pp., $17.95
How to Keep Your Honda ATC Alive (28-45-1) 236 pp., $14.95

Other Automotive Books

**The Greaseless Guide to Car Care Confidence: Take the Terror out of Talking
to Your Mechanic,** Mary Jackson
Teaches the reader about all of the basic systems of an automobile. (65-19-X)
200 pp., $14.95

Off-Road Emergency Repair & Survival, James Ristow
Glove compartment guide to troubleshooting, temporary repair, and survival.
(65-26-2) 150 pp., $9.95

Road & Track's Used Car Classics, edited by Peter Bohr
Features over 70 makes and models of enthusiast cars built between 1953 and
1979. (28-69-9) 272 pp., $12.95

Ordering Information

Fill in the order blank. Be sure to add up all of the subtotals at the bottom of the order form and give us the address whither your order is to be whisked.

Postage & Handling

Your books will be sent to you via UPS (for U.S. destinations), and you will receive them in approximately 10 days from the time that we receive your order. Include $2.75 for the first item ordered and $.50 for each additional item to cover shipping and handling costs. UPS shipments to post office boxes take longer to arrive; if possible, please give us a street address.

For airmail within the U.S., enclose $4.00 per book for shipping and handling.

All foreign orders will be shipped surface rate. Please enclose $3.00 for the first item and $1.00 for each additional item. Please inquire for airmail rates.

Method of Payment

Your order may be paid by check, money order, or credit card. We cannot be responsible for cash sent through the mail.

All payments must be made in U.S. dollars drawn on a U.S. bank. Canadian postal money orders in U.S. dollars are also acceptable.

For VISA, MasterCard, or American Express orders, use the order form or call (505)982-4078. Books ordered on American Express cards can be shipped only to the billing address of the cardholder. Sorry, no C.O.D.'s. Residents of sunny New Mexico, add 5.625% tax to the total.

Back Orders

We will back order all forthcoming and out-of-stock titles unless otherwise requested.

All prices subject to change without notice.

Address all orders and inquiries to: **John Muir Publications**
P.O. Box 613
Santa Fe, NM 87504   **(505)982-4078**

ITEM NO.			TITLE	EACH	QUAN.	TOTAL
		·				
		·				
		·				
		·				
		·				

Postage & handling (see ordering information)* _____

New Mexicans please add 5.625% tax _____

Total Amount Due _____

Credit Card Number: _____

Expiration Date: _____ Daytime telephone _____

Name _____

Address _____

City _____ State _____ Zip _____

Signature X _____

Required for Credit Card Purchases